BLUE-RIBBON
AFGHANS

Compiled and Edited by
Janica York

Library of Congress Catalog Number: 98-65197
Hardcover ISBN: 0-8487-1457-1
Softcover ISBN: 0-8487-1460-1
Manufactured in the United States of America
Seventh Printing 2001

Editor-in-Chief: Nancy Fitzpatrick Wyatt
Senior Crafts Editor: Susan Ramey Cleveland
Senior Editor, Editorial Services: Olivia Kindig Wells
Art Director: James Boone

Herrschners Blue-Ribbon Afghans

Editor: Janica York
Editorial Assistant: Allison Ingram
Copy Editor: L. Amanda Owens
Associate Art Director: Cynthia R. Cooper
Senior Designer: Larry Hunter
Illustrators: Barbara Ball, Anita Bice, Kelly Davis
Senior Photographer: John O'Hagan
Photo Stylist: Linda Baltzell Wright
Production Director: Phillip Lee
Associate Production Manager: Theresa L. Beste
Production Assistant: Faye Porter Bonner
Publishing Systems Administrator: Rick Tucker

We're Here for You!
   We at Oxmoor House are dedicated to serving you with reliable information that expands your imagination and enriches your life. We welcome your comments and suggestions. Please write us at:
   Oxmoor House, Inc.
   Editor, *Herrschners Blue-Ribbon Afghans*
   2100 Lakeshore Drive
   Birmingham, AL 35209
To order additional publications, call 1-205-877-6560.

Table of Contents

Afghans for All Occasions

Garden Rows	4
Groovy Granny	7
Sandy Shells	10
Country Quilt	12
Blue Star	16
Pinwheel	22
Memory Star	24
Textured Sampler	27
Pink Diamonds	30
Bluebirds and Bluebells	32
Floral Fantasy	37
Mum's the Word	40
Purple Starbursts	42
Fan-Stitch Favorite	44
Artful Aztec	46
Irish Trellis	50
Scalloped Ripple	52
Paisley Perfection	55
Afghan-Stitch Aran	58
Diamonds and Rings	61
Rippling Shells	64
Bargello Beauty	66
Christmas Celebration	70
Hearts and Flowers	73
Borderline	76
Lattice	80
Bright Ribbons	82
Cheyenne Chevron	84
Pretty in Pink	86
Hummingbirds	88
Tumbling Blocks	92
Cowboy Blues	94
Colorful Cables	97
Stained Glass	100
Heavenly Love	106
Giraffes	110

Afghans for Little Ones

White Shells	114
Tweed Stripes	116
Pink and Blue	118
Color Block	120
Tic-tac-toe	122
Spots and Stripes	126
Filet Hearts	129
Sherbet Stripes	132
Puffed Shells	134
Rainbow Ripple	136
Baby Blocks	139
Puffed Stripes	142
General Directions	144
Index	160

Editor's Note

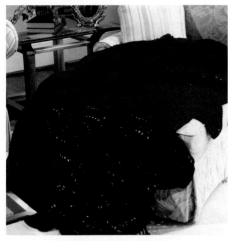

Pinwheel, page 22

Heavenly Love, page 106

Filet Hearts, page 129

Since 1991 Herrschners Grand National Afghan Contest has been the proving ground for some of the finest afghan designs in America. With competition categories for crocheted and knitted patterns for adults and babies, the award-winning afghans represent the diverse and masterful skills of stitchers from across the country. From traditional to trendy and classic to clever, each afghan features a special technique or a color combination that impressed national judges.

We've gathered four dozen of these winners in this one volume. You're sure to find designs just right for your home. There are afghans for all occasions and all ages.

We've designated each afghan as beginner, intermediate, or advanced so that you can choose the projects that are right for you. Of course, once you've mastered the basics, you'll be ready to move on to the next level. Look for the following symbols at the beginning of each set of directions.

Beginner

Intermediate

Advanced

We hope this collection of top-notch designs will inspire you to stitch some winners of your own.

If you would like more information about Herrschners Grand National Afghan Contest or if you would like to order supplies to make any of the afghans in this book, please contact Herrschners at 2800 Hoover Road, Stevens Point, Wisconsin, 54492, or call 1-800-441-0838, or visit the web site at http://www.herrschners.com.

AFGHANS FOR ALL OCCASIONS

Garden Rows

White paths between the rose-and-green flower blocks bring order to multicolored rows.

Materials

Worsted-weight acrylic yarn, approximately:
24 oz. (1,395 yd.) rose-and-green multicolored, MC
14 oz. (795 yd.) teal, A
16 oz. (905 yd.) white, B
Size G crochet hook or size to obtain gauge

Finished Size
Approximately 48" x 62"

Gauge
Ea Square = 6½"

Pattern Stitch
Cl: 3 dc in st or sp indicated.

Square (Make 36.)
With MC, ch 6, join with sl st to form ring.
Rnd 1 (rs): Ch 3 [counts as first dc throughout], (hdc, sc) in ring, * ch 3, (dc, hdc, sc) in ring; rep from * 4 times more, ch 3; join with sl st to top of beg ch-3; fasten off: 6 ch-3 sps.
Rnd 2: With rs facing, join A in any ch-3 sp with sl st, ch 1, sc in same sp, (ch 4, sc in next ch-3 sp) 5 times, ch 4; join with sl st to beg sc.
Rnd 3: Ch 3, (2 dc, ch 3, cl) in same st, sc in next ch-4 sp, * (cl, ch 3, cl) in next sc, sc in next ch-4 sp; rep from * around; join with sl st to top of beg ch-3; fasten off.
Rnd 4: With rs facing, join B in any ch-3 sp with sl st, ch 1, sc in same sp, * ch 3, dc in next sc, ch 3 **, sc in next ch-3 sp; rep from * around, ending last rep at **; join with sl st to beg sc.

Rnd 5: Ch 2 [counts as first hdc], * 3 sc in next ch-3 sp, hdc in next dc, (hdc, 2 dc) in next ch-3 sp, (2 tr, ch 3, 2 tr) in next dc [corner made], (2 dc, hdc) in next ch-3 sp **, hdc in next dc; rep from * around, ending last rep at **; join with sl st to top of beg ch-2; fasten off.
Rnd 6 (ws): With ws facing, join A in any corner ch-3 sp with sl st, ch 1, * (2 sc, ch 2, 2 sc) in same corner ch-3 sp, sc in next 15 sts; rep from * around; join with sl st to beg sc; fasten off.
Rnd 7 (rs): With rs facing, join MC in any corner ch-2 sp with sl st, ch 3, (2 dc, ch 3, cl) in same sp, (ch 1, sk 3 sc, cl in next sc) across to next corner ch-2 sp, ch 1, * (cl, ch 3, cl) in corner ch-2 sp, (ch 1, sk 3 sc, cl in next sc) across to next corner ch-2 sp; rep from * around, ch 1; join with sl st to top of beg ch-3; fasten off: 36 cls.

Horizontal Strip (Make 6.)
Join 2 Squares as folls: With rs tog, working through bk lps only, join MC in any corner ch-3 sp with sl st, ch 1, sc in same sp, sc in ea sc across to next corner ch-3 sp, sc in corner ch-3 sp; fasten off.
Rep to join 6 Squares.
Edging
Rnd 1 (rs): With rs facing, join MC in bottom right corner ch-3 sp with sl st, ch 3, (2 dc, ch 3, cl) in same sp, * (ch 1, cl in next ch-1 sp) across to next corner ch-3 sp, (cl, ch 3, cl) in corner ch-3 sp, ([ch 1, cl in next ch-1 sp] across to next joining, ch 1, cl in joining) 5 times, (ch 1, cl in

(continued)

next ch-1 sp) across to next corner ch-3 sp **, (cl, ch 3, cl) in corner ch-3 sp; rep from * around, ending last rep at **, ch 1; join with sl st to top of beg ch-3; fasten off: 88 cls.

Note: Beg working in rows.

Row 1 (rs): With rs facing and working along long edge of Strip, join A in corner with sl st, ch 4 [counts as first dc plus ch 1], * dc in center dc of next cl, ch 1 **, tr in center dc of next cl 2 rnds below, ch 1; rep from * across, ending last rep at **, dc in corner ch-3 sp; fasten off.

Row 2: With rs facing, join B in 3rd ch of beg ch-4 of row 1 with sl st, ch 1, sc in same st, * dc in first dc of next cl 2 rows below, sc in next dc of row 1 **, dc in 3rd dc of cl 2 rows below, sc in next tr of row 1; rep

from * across, ending last rep at **; fasten off.

Rep rows 1 and 2 along bottom edge of Strip.

Assembly

Join 2 Strips as folls: With rs tog working through bk lps only, join MC in any corner ch-3 sp with sl st, ch 1, sc in same sp, sc in ea sc across to next corner ch-3 sp, sc in corner ch-3 sp; fasten off.

Rep to join 6 Strips.

Border

Rnd 1 (rs): With rs facing, join MC in top right corner with sl st, ch 3, (2 dc, ch 3, cl) in same corner, * (ch 1, sk 3 sts, cl in next st) across to next corner, ch 1, (cl, ch 3, cl) in corner, ([ch 1, cl in next ch-1 sp]

across to next joining, ch 1, cl in joining) 5 times, (ch 1, cl in next ch-1 sp) across to next corner ch-3 sp **, (cl, ch 3, cl) in corner ch-3 sp; rep from * around, ending last rep at **, ch 1; join with sl st to top of beg ch-3.

Rnds 2–6: Sl st in next 2 dc and in corner ch-3 sp, ch 3, (2 dc, ch 3, cl) in same sp, (ch 1, cl in next ch-1 sp) across to next corner ch-3 sp, * ch 1, (cl, ch 3, cl) in corner ch-3 sp, (ch 1, cl in next ch-1 sp) across to next corner ch-3 sp; rep from * around; ch 1; join with sl st to top of beg ch-3; fasten off after last rnd.

Rnd 7: With rs facing, join A in any corner ch-3 sp with sl st, * ch 1, (sc, ch 3, sc) in corner ch-3 sp, (ch 1, sc in center dc of next cl, ch 1, sc in next ch-1 sp) across to next corner ch-3 sp; rep from * around, ch 1; join with sl st to beg sc.

Rnd 8: Sl st in corner ch-3 sp, * ch 1, (sc, ch 3, sc) in corner ch-3 sp, (ch 1, sc in next ch-1 sp) across to next corner ch-3 sp; rep from * around, ch 1; join with sl st to top of beg sc; fasten off.

Rnd 9: With rs facing, join MC in any corner ch-3 sp with sl st, ch 1, * (sc, ch 3, dc, hdc, sc) in corner ch-3 sp, (sk next ch-1 sp, [sc, ch 3, dc, hdc, sc] in next ch-1 sp) across to next corner ch-3 sp; rep from * around; join with sl st to beg sc; fasten off.

Afghan by Sarah Karnes
Wyoming, Michigan

Groovy Granny

Create a funky new look with a traditional stitch. The secret lies in the unusual—but easy—joining technique.

Materials

Worsted-weight acrylic yarn, approximately:
- 12 oz. (680 yd.) black, MC
- 6 oz. (340 yd.) light coral, A
- 16 oz. (905 yd.) coral, B
- 18 oz. (1,020 yd.) jade, C
- 8 oz. (455 yd.) mint, D
- 8 oz. (455 yd.) pale green, E
- 8 oz. (455 yd.) lilac, F
- 8 oz. (455 yd.) lavender, G
- 8 oz. (455 yd.) purple, H
- Size G crochet hook or size to obtain gauge
- Yarn needle

Finished Size

Approximately 58" x 72½"

Gauge

Granny Square = 6½"

Pattern Stitches

Beg cl: (Ch 3, 2 dc, ch 2, 3 dc, ch 1) in sp indicated.
Corner cl: (3 dc, ch 2, 3 dc, ch 1) in sp indicated.
FPtr: Yo twice, insert hook from front to back around st indicated, yo and pull up lp, (yo and pull through 2 lps) 3 times.

Granny Square (Make 20.)

With A, ch 5, join with sl st to form ring.
Rnd 1 (rs): Ch 3 [counts as first dc throughout], 2 dc in ring, ch 2, (3 dc in ring, ch 2) 3 times; join with sl st to top of beg ch-3.
Rnd 2: Ch 4 [counts as first dc plus ch 1 throughout], (corner cl in next ch-2 sp) 3 times, (3 dc, ch 2, dc) in next ch-2 sp; join with sl st to 3rd ch of beg ch-4: 8 cls.
Rnd 3: Ch 3, 2 dc in first ch-1 sp, ch 1, * corner cl in next ch-2 sp, 3 dc in next ch-1 sp, ch 1; rep from * twice more, corner cl in next ch-2 sp; join with sl st to top of beg ch-3; fasten off: 12 cls.
Rnd 4: With rs facing, join B with

sl st in any corner ch-2 sp, beg cl in same sp,* (3 dc in next ch-1 sp, ch 1) twice, corner cl in next ch-2 sp; rep from * twice more, (3 dc in next ch-1 sp, ch 1) twice; join with sl st to top of beg ch-3: 16 cls.
Rnd 5: Ch 4, * corner cl in next ch-2 sp, (3 dc in next ch-1 sp, ch 1) 3 times; rep from * twice more, corner cl in next ch-2 sp, (3 dc in next ch-1 sp, ch 1) twice, 2 dc in next ch-1 sp; join with sl st to 3rd ch of beg ch-4: 20 cls.
Rnd 6: Ch 3, 2 dc in first ch-1 sp, ch 1, * corner cl in next ch-2 sp, (3 dc in next ch-1 sp, ch 1) 4 times; rep from * twice more, corner cl in next ch-2 sp, (3 dc in next ch-1 sp, ch 1) 3 times; join with sl st to top of beg ch-3; fasten off: 24 cls.

Strip (Make 4.)

Rnd 1 (rs): With rs facing, join C in center ch-1 sp of any side of 1 Square with sl st, ch 3, 2 dc in same sp, ch 1, * (3 dc in next ch-1 sp, ch 1) twice, corner cl in next ch-2 sp, (3 dc in next ch-1 sp, ch 1) 5 times, corner cl in next ch-2 sp, 3 dc in next ch-1 sp, ch 1, 3 dc in next ch-1 sp, tr in next ch-1 sp, ch 27, tr in center ch-1 sp of any side of next Square; rep from * 3 times [5 Squares joined]; (3 dc in next ch-1 sp, ch 1) twice, (corner cl in next ch-2 sp, [3 dc in next ch-1 sp, ch 1] 5 times) 3 times, † corner cl in next ch-2 sp, 3 dc in next ch-1 sp, ch 1, 3 dc in next ch-1 sp, tr in next ch-1 sp, (dc in next 3 chs, ch 1, sk next ch) 6 times, dc in last 3 chs, tr in center ch-1 sp of next Square, (3 dc in next ch-1 sp, ch 1) twice, corner cl in next ch-2 sp, (3 dc in next ch-1 sp, ch 1) 5 times; rep from † 3 times, corner cl in next ch-2 sp, (3 dc in next ch-1 sp, ch 1) twice, sl to top of beg ch-3.
Rnd 2: Sl st in next 2 dc, sl st in next ch-1 sp, ch 3, 2 dc in same sp, ch 1, * ([3 dc in next ch-1 sp, ch 1] across to corner ch-2 sp, corner cl in

ch-2 sp) twice, (3 dc in next ch-1 sp, ch 1) across to ch-1 sp before next tr, 3 dc in same ch-1 sp, FPtr around next tr, (3 dc in next ch-1 sp, ch 1) across to ch-1 sp before next tr, 3 dc in same ch-1 sp, FPtr around next tr **; rep from * 3 times, ([3 dc in next ch-1 sp, ch 1] across to corner ch-2 sp, corner cl in ch-2 sp) 4 times, (3 dc in next ch-1 sp, ch 1) across to ch-1 sp before next tr, 3 dc in same ch-1 sp, FPtr around next tr, (3 dc in next ch-1 sp, ch 1) across to ch-1 sp before next tr, 3 dc in same ch-1 sp, FPtr around next tr; rep from * to ** 3 times, ([3 dc in next ch-1 sp, ch 1] across to corner ch-2 sp) twice, (3 dc in next ch-1 sp, ch 1) across to beg ch-3; join with sl st to top of beg ch-3; fasten off.
Rnd 3: With rs facing, join D in last ch-sp worked with sl st, ch 3, 2 dc in same sp, ch 1, * ([3 dc in next ch-1 sp, ch 1] across to corner ch-2 sp, corner cl in ch-2 sp) twice, (3 dc in next ch-1 sp, ch 1) across to ch-1 sp before next FPtr, 3 dc in same ch-1 sp, FPtr around next FPtr, (3 dc in next ch-1 sp, ch 1) across to ch-1 sp before next FPtr, 3 dc in same ch-1 sp, FPtr around next FPtr **; rep from * 3 times, ([3 dc in next ch-1 sp, ch 1] across to corner ch-2 sp, corner cl in ch-2 sp) 4 times, (3 dc in next ch-1 sp, ch 1) across to ch-1 sp before next FPtr, 3 dc in same ch-1 sp, FPtr around next FPtr, (3 dc in next ch-1 sp, ch 1) across to ch-1 sp before next tr, 3 dc in same ch-1 sp, FPtr around next tr; rep from * to ** 3 times, ([3 dc in next ch-1 sp, ch 1] across to corner ch-2 sp) twice, (3 dc in next ch-1 sp, ch 1) across to beg ch-3; join with sl st to top of beg ch-3; fasten off.
Rnd 4: With E, rep rnd 3.
Rnd 5: With F, rep rnd 3.
Rnd 6: With G, rep rnd 3.
Rnd 7: With H, rep rnd 3.
Rnd 8: With rs facing, join MC in last ch-sp worked with sl st, ch 3,

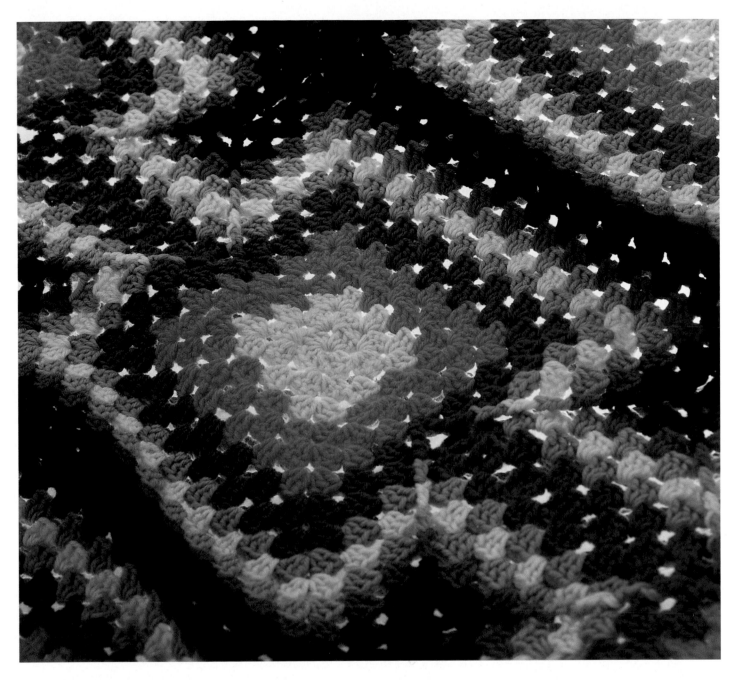

2 dc in same sp, ch 1, ([3 dc in next ch-1 sp, ch 1] across to corner ch-2 sp, corner cl in ch-2 sp) twice, * (3 dc in next ch-1 sp, ch 1) across to ch-1 sp before next FPtr, 3 dc in same ch-1 sp, FPtr around next 2 FPtr, (3 dc in next ch-1 sp, sl st in corresponding ch-1 sp on prev Square, ch 1) across to corner ch-2 sp, 3 dc in ch-2 sp, sl st in corresponding ch-2 sp on prev Square, ch 2, 3 dc in same ch-2 sp, (3 dc in next ch-1 sp, ch 1) across to next corner ch-2 sp, corner cl in ch-2 sp **; rep from * 3 times, ([3 dc in next ch-1 sp, ch 1] across to next corner ch-2 sp, corner cl in ch-2 sp) twice; rep from * to ** 4 times, (3 dc in next ch-1 sp, ch 1) across to beg ch-3; join with sl st to top of beg ch-3; fasten off.

Assembly

With ws tog and using MC, join Strips as folls: Sc in bottom ch-2 sp, * ch 4 loosely, sc in next ch-1 sp; rep from * across to last ch-2 sp, sc in last ch-2 sp; fasten off.

Border

Rnd 1 (rs): With rs facing, join MC in any corner with sl st, ch 3, (2 dc, ch 2, 3 dc) in same sp, * ([3 dc in next ch-1 sp, ch 1] across to Strip joining, dc in sp before joining, dc in joining, dc in sp after joining) across to next corner **, corner cl in corner; rep from * around, ending last rep at **; join with sl st to top of beg ch-3; fasten off.
Rnd 2: With C, rep rnd 1.

Afghan by Kathy Blakely
Ririe, Idaho

Sandy Shells

Simple double-crochet shells worked in stripes of
sea and sand colors are as soothing as ocean waves
lapping the shore.

Materials

Chunky-weight acrylic yarn,
approximately:
42 oz. (1,680 yd.) cream, MC
15 oz. (600 yd.) green, A
15 oz. (600 yd.) tan, B
Size J crochet hook or size to
obtain gauge

Finished Size

Approximately 44" x 69", without
fringe

Gauge

4 shells = 3½" and 8 rows = 4"

Pattern Stitch

Shell: 3 dc in st indicated.

Note: To change colors, work last yo
of st with new color, dropping prev
color to ws of work. Do not carry
yarn across row.

With MC, ch 157.
Row 1 (rs): Dc in 4th ch from hook,
sk next 2 chs, * shell in next ch,
sk next 2 chs; rep from * across to
last ch, 2 dc in last ch: 50 shells and
2 half-shells.
Row 2: Ch 1, turn; sc in first dc,
ch 2, (sc in top of next shell, ch 2)
across, sc in top of beg ch-3.
Row 3: Ch 3, turn; dc in first sc,
shell in next sc and in ea sc across to
last sc, 2 dc in last dc.
Rows 4–138: Rep rows 2 and 3
alternately, ending with row 2 and
foll color sequence: 7 rows MC,
* 4 rows A, 4 rows MC, 10 rows B,
4 rows MC, 4 rows A **, 20 rows
MC; rep from * once, then rep from

* to ** once, 10 rows MC; do not
fasten off.

Border

Rnd 1 (rs): Ch 1, turn; 2 sc in same
sc, * (2 sc in next ch-2 sp, sc in next
sc) across to next corner **, 3 sc in
corner, sc evenly across to next corner, 3 sc in corner; rep from * to **
once, sc in corner; join with sl st to
beg sc.
Rnd 2: Ch 1, do not turn; working
from left to right, sc in joining,
* ch 1, sk next sc, sc in next sc; rep
from * around; join with sl st to
beg sc; fasten off.

Fringe

For ea tassel, referring to page 159
of General Directions, cut 5 (14")
lengths of MC; working across short
ends, knot 1 tassel in ea ch-1 sp.

*Afghan by Monica Kancel-Costello
Hannibal, Ohio*

Country Quilt

Show pride in your heritage with classic quilt blocks in patriotic colors. The pattern is worked in sportweight yarn, so each chart square represents two stitches, not one.

Materials

Sportweight acrylic yarn, approximately:
22 oz. (2,200 yd.) cream, MC
8 oz. (800 yd.) burgundy, A
20 oz. (2,000 yd.) navy, B
Size D crochet hook or size to obtain gauge
Yarn needle

Finished Size

Approximately 45" x 66"

Gauge

25 dc and 12 rows = 4"

Note: To change colors, work last yo of prev st with new color, dropping prev color to ws of work. Do not carry yarn across row.

Panel 1

With B, ch 58.
Row 1 (rs): Referring to *Chart 1* on page 14, dc in 4th ch from hook and in ea ch across: 56 dc.
Rows 2–4: Ch 3 [counts as first dc throughout], turn; dc in next dc and in ea dc across; change to A in last st of last row: 56 dc.
Rows 5–8: Ch 3, turn; dc in next dc and in ea dc across.
Row 9: Ch 3, turn; dc in next 7 dc, change to B, dc in next 18 dc, change to A, dc in next 4 dc, change to B, dc in next 18 dc, change to MC, dc in last 8 dc.
Rows 10–32: Cont foll *Chart 1* as est; change to B in last st of last row.
Rows 33–64: Foll *Chart 2* on page 14; change to B in last st of last row.
Rows 65–96: Foll *Chart 3* on page

14; change to B in last st of last row.
Rows 97–128: Foll *Chart 4* on page 14; change to B in last st of last row.
Rows 129–160: Foll *Chart 1;* change to B in last st of last row.
Rows 161–192: Foll *Chart 2;* change to B in last st of last row.
Rows 193–196: Rep row 2, 4 times, do not change colors in last st of last row; fasten off.

Edging

Row 1 (rs): With rs facing, join B in bottom right corner with sl st, ch 1, sc in same st, work 2 sc in end of ea row across.
Rows 2–4: Ch 3, turn; dc in next sc and in ea sc across; fasten off after last row.
Row 5 (rs): With rs facing, join B in top left corner with sl st, ch 1, sc in same st, work 2 sc in end of ea row across.
Rows 6–8: Rep rows 2–4 once.

Panel 2

With B, ch 58.
Row 1 (rs): Referring to *Chart 2*, dc in 4th ch from hook and in ea ch across: 56 dc.
Rows 2–32: Cont foll *Chart 2* as est; change to B in last st of last row.
Rows 33–64: Foll *Chart 3;* change to B in last st of last row.
Rows 65–96: Foll *Chart 4;* change to B in last st of last row.
Rows 97–128: Foll *Chart 1;* change to B in last st of last row.
Rows 129–160: Foll *Chart 2;* change to B in last st of last row.
Rows 161–192: Foll *Chart 3;* change to B in last st of last row.
Rows 193–196: Rep row 2, 4 times, do not change colors in last st of last row; fasten off.

Edging

Row 1 (rs): With rs facing, join B in bottom right corner with sl st, ch 1, sc in same st, work 2 sc in end of ea row across.
Rows 2–4: Ch 3, turn; dc in next sc and in ea sc across; fasten off after last row.
Row 5 (rs): With rs facing, join B in top left corner with sl st, ch 1, sc in same st, work 2 sc in end of ea row across; fasten off.

Panel 3

With B, ch 58.
Row 1 (rs): Referring to *Chart 3,* dc in 4th ch from hook and in ea ch across: 56 dc.
Rows 2–32: Cont foll *Chart 3* as est; change to B in last st of last row.
Rows 33–64: Foll *Chart 4;* change to B in last st of last row.
Rows 65–96: Foll *Chart 1;* change to B in last st of last row.
Rows 97–128: Foll *Chart 2;* change to B in last st of last row.
Rows 129–160: Foll *Chart 3;* change to B in last st of last row.
Rows 161–192: Foll *Chart 4;* change to B in last st of last row.
Rows 193–196: Rep row 2, 4 times, do not change colors in last st of last row; fasten off.

Edging

Row 1 (rs): With rs facing, join B in bottom right corner with sl st, ch 1, sc in same st, work 2 sc in end of ea row across.
Rows 2–4: Ch 3, turn; dc in next sc and in ea sc across; fasten off after last row.

(continued)

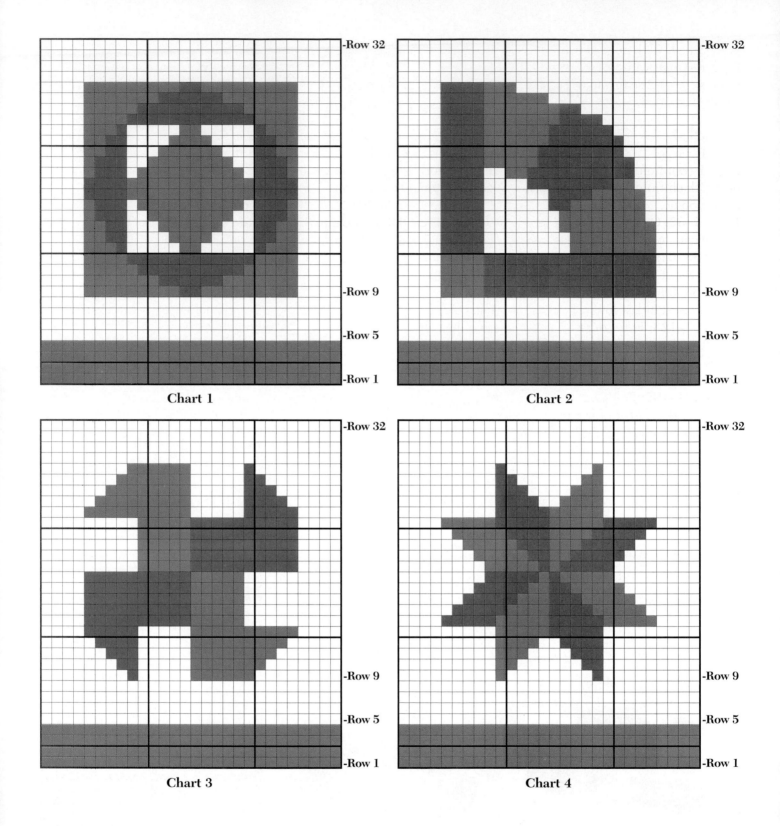

Chart 1

Chart 2

Chart 3

Chart 4

Key

Ea square = 2 dc

☐ MC

■ A

■ B

Row 5 (rs): With rs facing, join B in top left corner with sl st, ch 1, sc in same st, work 2 sc in end of ea row across; fasten off.

Panel 4

With B, ch 58.

Row 1 (rs): Referring to **Chart 4,** dc in 4th ch from hook and in ea ch across: 56 dc.

Rows 2–32: Cont foll **Chart 4** as est; change to B in last st of last row.

Rows 33–64: Foll **Chart 1;** change to B in last st of last row.

Rows 65–96: Foll **Chart 2;** change to B in last st of last row.

Rows 97–128: Foll **Chart 3;** change to B in last st of last row.

Rows 129–160: Foll **Chart 4;** change to B in last st of last row.

Rows 161–192: Foll **Chart 1;** change to B in last st of last row.

Rows 193–196: Rep row 2, 4 times, do not change colors in last st of last row; fasten off.

Edging

Row 1 (rs): With rs facing, join B in bottom right corner with sl st, ch 1, sc in same st, work 2 sc in end of ea row across.

Rows 2–4: Ch 3, turn; dc in next sc and in ea sc across; fasten off after last row.

Row 5 (rs): With rs facing, join B in top left corner with sl st, ch 1, sc in same st, work 2 sc in end of ea row across; fasten off.

Granny Square (Make 35.)

With A, ch 5, join with sl st to form ring.

Rnd 1 (rs): Ch 2 [counts as first hdc], 2 hdc in ring, ch 3, (3 hdc in ring, ch 3) 3 times; join with sl st to top of beg ch-2: 12 hdc.

Rnd 2: Ch 3, dc in next 2 hdc, (2 dc, ch 3, 2 dc) in next ch-3 sp, * dc in next 3 hdc, (2 dc, ch 3, 2 dc) in next ch-3 sp; rep from * 3 times; join with sl st to top of beg ch-3; fasten off.

Panel Assembly

With ws facing, referring to **Assembly Diagram**, and using B, whipstitch Panels tog.

Border

Row 1 (rs): With rs facing, join B in top right corner with sl st, ch 1, sc in same st and in ea st across; fasten off.

Row 2 (rs): With rs facing, join B in bottom left corner with sl st, ch 1, sc in same st and in ea st across; fasten off.

Note: Beg working in rnds.

Rnd 1 (rs): With rs facing, join MC in any corner with sl st, ch 3, 5 dc in same corner, dc evenly across to next corner, * 5 dc in corner, dc evenly across to next corner; rep from * around; join with sl st to top of beg ch-3.

Rnd 2: Ch 3, dc in next dc and ea dc across to corner, * 5 dc in corner, dc in ea dc across to next corner; rep from * around; join with sl st to top of beg ch-3; fasten off.

Assembly

Referring to **Assembly Diagram** and using A, whipstitch Granny Squares to afghan.

Afghan by Laurie Halama
Independence, Wisconsin

1   2   3   4

Assembly Diagram

Blue Star

This stellar afghan requires several steps, but the stitches are easy granny-square variations. Start with basic granny squares and then work outward from the center medallion.

Materials ⬤ ⬤ ⬤

Worsted-weight acrylic yarn, approximately:
- 17½ oz. (990 yd.) light blue, MC
- 10½ oz. (595 yd.) blue, A
- 17½ oz. (990 yd.) navy, B
- 17½ oz. (990 yd.) cream, C
- 14 oz. (700 yd.) blue-and-cream multicolored, D

Size G crochet hook or size to obtain gauge
Yarn needle

Finished Size

Approximately 60" x 60"

Gauge

Granny Square = 7"

Pattern Stitch

Cl: 3 dc in sp indicated.

Granny Block 1 (Make 8.)

Center Square
With C, ch 5, join with sl st to form ring.
Rnd 1 (ws): Ch 3 [counts as first dc throughout], 2 dc in ring, ch 2 (cl in ring, ch 2) 3 times; join with sl st to top of beg ch-3.
Rnd 2 (rs): Turn; sl st in first ch-2 sp, ch 3, 2 dc in same sp, ch 1, * (cl, ch 2, cl) in next ch-2 sp, ch 1; rep from * twice more, cl in next ch-2 sp, ch 2; join with sl st to top of beg ch-3; fasten off.
Note: Side and Corner Squares are joined to Center Square as they are made.
Side Square (Make 4.)
With A, ch 5, join with sl st to form ring.

Rnd 1 (ws): Ch 3, 2 dc in ring, ch 2, (cl in ring, ch 2) 3 times; join with sl st to top of beg ch-3.
Rnd 2 (rs): Turn; sl st in first ch-2 sp, ch 3, 2 dc in same sp, ch 1, * cl in next corner ch-2 sp of Side Square, sc in corner ch-2 sp of Center Square, cl in same ch-2 sp on Side Square **, sc in next ch-1 sp of Center Square; rep from * to ** once, ch 1, (cl, ch 2, cl) in next ch-2 sp, ch 1, cl in next ch-2 sp, ch 2; join with sl st to top of beg ch-3; fasten off.
Corner Square (Make 4.)
With D, ch 5, join with sl st to form ring.
Rnd 1 (ws): Ch 3, 2 dc in ring, ch 2, (cl in ring, ch 2) 3 times; join with sl st to top of beg ch-3.
Rnd 2 (rs): Turn; sl st in first ch-2 sp, ch 3, 2 dc in same sp, ch 1, cl in next corner ch-2 sp, sc in corner ch-2 sp of Side Square, cl in same ch-2 sp on Corner Square, sc in next ch-1 sp of Side Square, cl in next corner ch-2 sp of Corner Square, sc in corner ch-2 sp of Center Square, cl in same ch-2 sp on Corner Square, sc in next ch-1 sp of next Side Square, cl in next corner ch-2 sp of Corner Square, sc in corner ch-2 sp of Side Square, cl in same ch-2 sp of Corner Square, ch 1, cl in next ch-2 sp, ch 2; join with sl st to top of beg ch-3; fasten off.
Edging (for 4 blocks only)
With rs facing, join B with sl st in any corner ch-2 sp, ch 1, sc in same sp, work 23 sc evenly sp across to next corner, 3 sc in corner, work 23 sc evenly sp across to next corner, sc in corner; fasten off: 51 sc.

Granny Block 2 (Make 4.)

Center Square
With C, work as for Granny Block 1.
Side Square
With D, work as for Granny Block 1.
Corner Square
With A, work as for Granny Block 1.
Edging (for 4 blocks only)
Work as for Granny Block 1.

Granny Block 3 (Make 8.)

Center Square
With A, work as for Granny Block 1.
Side Square
With C, work as for Granny Block 1.
Corner Square
With D, work as for Granny Block 1.
Edging
Do not edge.

Note: When making corners for Granny Block 4, use only the lighter sections of the multicolored yarn by cutting out the darker sections. This keeps the overall square lighter.

Granny Block 4 (Make 8.)

Center Square
With MC, work as for Granny Block 1.
Side Square
With C, work as for Granny Block 1.
Corner Square
With D, work as for Granny Block 1.
Edging
Do not edge.

Star

Center
With C, ch 5, join with sl st to form ring.
Rnd 1 (rs): Ch 4 [counts as first dc

(continued)

plus ch 1 throughout], (dc, ch 1) 11 times in ring; join with sl st to 3rd ch of beg ch-4: 12 dc.

Rnd 2: Ch 3, dc in first ch-1 sp, * 3 dc in next ch-1 sp, 2 dc in next ch-1 sp; rep from * 4 times more, 3 dc in next ch-1 sp; join with sl st in top of beg ch-3: 30 dc.

Rnd 3: Ch 3, dc in next dc, * (dc, ch 2, dc) in next dc, dc in next 3 dc **, (dc, ch 2, dc) in next dc, dc in next dc, 2 dc in next dc; rep from * twice more, then rep from * to ** once, dc in next dc, ch 2, dc in next 2 dc; join with sl st to top of beg ch-2: 40 dc and 8 ch-2 sps.

Rnd 4: Ch 1, (cl, ch 2, cl) in next ch-2 sp, * sk next 2 dc, sc in next dc, (cl, ch 2, cl) in next ch-2 sp; rep from * 6 times more; join with sc to beg ch-1.

Rnd 5: Ch 1, * sc in next dc, hdc in next dc, dc in next dc, (2 dc, ch 2, 2 dc) in next ch-2 sp, dc in next dc, hdc in next dc, sc in next dc, sk next sc; rep from * 7 times more; join with sl st to beg sc.

Rnd 6: Ch 3, * sk next hdc, dc in next dc, ch 1, (cl, ch 3, cl) in next ch-2 sp, ch 1, sk next 3 dc, dc in next hdc **, sk next sc, dc in next sc; rep from * 6 times more, then rep from * to ** once; join with sl st to top of beg ch-3.

Rnd 7: Sl st in next dc and next ch-1 sp, ch 3, 2 dc in same sp, * ch 1, (cl, ch 3, cl) in next ch-3 sp, ch 1 **, (cl in next ch-1 sp) twice; rep from * 6 times more, then rep from * to ** once, cl in next ch-1 sp; join with sl st to top of beg ch-3.

Rnd 8: Ch 4, * cl in next ch-1 sp, ch 1, (cl, ch 3, cl) in next ch-3 sp, ch 1, cl in next ch-1 sp **, dc in sp bet next 2 cls, ch 1; rep from * 6 times more, then rep from * to ** once; join with sl st to 3rd ch of beg ch-3.

Rnd 9: Ch 4, * sk next cl, cl in next ch-1 sp, ch 1, (3 tr, ch 4, 3 tr) in next ch-3 sp, ch 1, cl in next ch-1 sp, ch 1, sk next cl **, dc in next dc, ch 1; rep from * 6 times more, then

rep from * to ** once; join with sl st to 3rd ch of beg ch-3; fasten off C.

Rnd 10 (rs): Join A with sl st in prev joining, ch 3, * dc in next ch-1 sp, ch 1, cl in next ch-1 sp, ch 1, (3 tr, ch 4, 3 tr) in next ch-4 sp, ch 1, cl in next ch-1 sp, ch 1, dc in next ch-1 sp **, dc in next dc; rep from * 6 times more, then rep from * to ** once; join with sl st to top of beg ch-3.

Rnd 11: Ch 1, sc in same st, * ch 1, sc in next ch-1 sp, ch 1, cl in next ch-1 sp, ch 1, (3 tr, ch 4, 3 tr) in next ch-4 sp, ch 1, cl in next ch-1 sp, ch 1, sc in next ch-1 sp, ch 1, sk next dc **, sc in next dc; rep from * 6 times, then rep from * to **once; join with sl st to top of beg sc; fasten off A.

Rnd 12 (rs): Join B with sl st in ch-1 sp after prev joining, ch 1, sc in same sp, * ch 1, cl in next ch-1 sp, ch 1, (2 dc, ch 1, 2 dc) in next ch-1 sp, ch 1, (2 dc, ch 1, 2 tr, ch 5, 2 tr, ch 1, 2 dc) in next ch-4 sp, ch 1, (2 dc, ch 1, 2 dc) in next ch-1 sp, ch 1, cl in next ch-1 sp **, (ch 1, sc in next ch-1 sp) twice; rep from * 6 times more, then rep from * to ** once; ch 1, sc in next ch-1 sp, ch 1; join with sl st to beg sc.

Rnd 13: Sl st in next ch-1 sp, ch 2, hdc in same sp, * ch 1, (2 hdc in next ch-1 sp, ch 1) twice, (cl in next ch-1 sp, ch 1) twice, (2 dc, ch 1, 2 tr, ch 5, 2 tr, ch 1, 2 dc) in next ch-5 sp, ch 1, (cl in next ch-1 sp, ch 1) twice, (2 hdc in next ch-1 sp, ch 1) 3 times, sc in next ch-1 sp, ch 1 **, 2 hdc in next ch-1 sp; rep from * 6 times more, then rep from * to ** once; join with sl st to top of beg ch-2; fasten off.

Note: You will need 4 ea of Granny Blocks 1 and 2 with edging. Alternate Granny Blocks 1 and 2 as you join them to Star.

Assembly

Join B in any ch-5 sp of Star with sl st, ch 5; with ws tog, * sc in first sc of edging of Granny Block, ch 1, 2 tr in same ch-5 sp of Star, sk 2 sc

of Block, sc in next sc of Block, 2 dc in same ch-5 sp of Star, sk 2 sc of Block, sc in next sc of Block, (cl in next ch-1 sp of Star, sk 2 sc of Block, sc in next sc of Block) 5 times, dc in next ch-1 sp of Star, sk 2 sc of Block, sc in next sc of Block, (dc in next ch-1 sp of Star, sc in next sc of Block) twice, dc in next ch-1 sp of Star, sk 2 sc of Block, sc in next sc of Block, (cl in next ch-1 sp of Star, sk 2 sc of Block, sc in next sc of Block) 5 times, 2 dc in next ch-5 sp of Star, sk 2 sc of Square, sc in next sc of Block **, 2 tr in same ch-5 sp of Star, sc in last sc of Block; rep from * 6 times, then rep from * to ** once, tr in same ch-5 sp of Star, sc in last sc of Block; join with sl st to 4th ch of beg ch-5; fasten off.

Border

Rnd 1 (rs): With rs facing, join MC with sl st in corner ch-2 sp of any Block [point], ch 1, 2 sc in same sp, * work 28 sc evenly sp across to Star joining, sc in joining, work 28 sc evenly sp across to next corner ch-2 sp **, 3 sc in corner; rep from * 6 times, then rep from * to ** once; sc in beg ch-2 sp; join with sl st to beg sc: 480 sc.

Rnd 2: Ch 5 [counts as first dc plus ch-2], * (sk next sc, dc in next 3 sc, ch 1) 15 times, ch 2; rep from * 6 times, (sk next sc, dc in next 3 sc, ch 1) 14 times, sk next sc, dc in next 2 dc; join with sl st to 3rd ch of beg ch-5: 360 dc.

Rnd 3: Ch 3, (2 dc, ch 2, cl) in same ch-2 sp, * ch 1, (cl in next ch-1 sp, ch 1) 6 times, dc in next ch-1 sp, sk next dc, dc in next dc, sk next dc, dc in next ch-1 sp, ch 1, (cl in next ch-1 sp, ch 1) 6 times **, (cl, ch 2, cl) in next ch-2 sp; rep from * 6 times, then rep from * to ** once; join with sl st to top of beg ch-3.

Rnd 4: Sl st in next 2 dc, sl st in next ch-2 sp, ch 3, (2 dc, ch 2, cl) in same ch-2 sp, * ch 1, (cl in next ch-1 sp, ch 1) 14 times **, (cl, ch 2, cl) in next ch-2 sp; rep from * 6

times, then rep from * to ** once; join with sl st to top of beg ch-3.

Rnd 5: Sl st in next 2 dc, sl st in next ch-2 sp, ch 3, (2 dc, ch 2, cl) in same ch-2 sp, * ch 1, (cl in next ch-1 sp, ch 1) 7 times, dc in next ch-1 sp, ch 1, (cl in next ch-1 sp, ch 1) 7 times **, (cl, ch 2, cl) in next ch-2 sp; rep from * 6 times, then rep from * to ** once; join with sl st to top of beg ch-3.

Rnd 6: Sl st in next 2 dc, sl st in next ch-2 sp, ch 3, (2 dc, ch 2, cl) in same ch-2 sp, * ch 1, (cl in next ch-1 sp, ch 1) 7 times, dc in next ch-1 sp, dc in next dc, dc in next ch-1 sp, ch 1, (cl in next ch-1 sp, ch 1) 7 times **,

(cl, ch 2, cl) in next ch-2 sp; rep from * 6 times, then rep from * to ** once; join with sl st to top of beg ch-3.

Rnd 7: Sl st in next 2 dc, sl st in next ch-2 sp, ch 3, (2 dc, ch 2, cl) in same ch-2 sp, * ch 1, (cl in next ch-1 sp, ch 1) 7 times, dc in next ch-1 sp, sk next dc, dc in next dc, sk next dc, dc in next ch-1 sp, ch 1, (cl in next ch-1 sp, ch 1) 7 times **, (cl, ch 2, cl) in next ch-2 sp; rep from * 6 times, then rep from * to ** once; join with sl st to top of beg ch-3.

Rnd 8: Sl st in next 2 dc, sl st in next ch-2 sp, ch 3, (2 dc, ch 2, cl) in same ch-2 sp, * ch 1, (cl in next

ch-1 sp, ch 1) 16 times **, (cl, ch 2, cl) in next ch-2 sp; rep from * 6 times, then rep from * to ** once; join with sl st to top of beg ch-3.

Rnd 9: Sl st in next 2 dc, sl st in next ch-2 sp, ch 3, (2 dc, ch 2, cl) in same ch-2 sp, * ch 1, (cl in next ch-1 sp, ch 1) 8 times, dc in next ch-1 sp, ch 1, (cl in next ch-1 sp, ch 1) 8 times **, (cl, ch 2, cl) in next ch-2 sp; rep from * 6 times, then rep from * to ** once; join with sl st to top of beg ch-3.

Rnd 10: Sl st in next 2 dc, sl st in next ch-2 sp, ch 3, (2 dc, ch 2, cl) in

(continued)

same ch-2 sp, * ch 1, (cl in next ch-1 sp, ch 1) 8 times, dc in next ch-1 sp, dc in next dc, dc in next ch-1 sp, ch 1, (cl in next ch-1 sp, ch 1) 8 times **, (cl, ch 2, cl) in next ch-2 sp; rep from * 6 times, then rep from * to ** once; join with sl st to top of beg ch-3.

Rnd 11: Sl st in next 2 dc, sl st in next ch-2 sp, ch 3, (2 dc, ch 2, cl) in same ch-2 sp, * ch 1, (cl in next ch-1 sp, ch 1) 8 times, dc in next ch-1 sp, sk next dc, dc in next dc, sk next dc, dc in next ch-1 sp, ch 1, (cl in next ch-1 sp, ch 1) 8 times **, (cl, ch 2, cl) in next ch-2 sp; rep from * 6 times, then rep from * to ** once; join with sl st to top of beg ch-3; fasten off.

Wedge (Make 8.)
With B, ch 4, join with sl st to form ring.

Row 1 (rs): Ch 3, (dc, ch 1, 2 dc) in ring: 4 dc.

Row 2: Ch 3, turn; dc in next dc, (dc, ch 1, dc) in ch-1 sp, dc in next 2 dc: 6 dc.

Row 3: Ch 3, turn; dc in next 2 dc and in ch-1 sp, ch 1, dc in next 3 dc: 7 dc.

Row 4: Ch 3, turn; dc in next 2 dc, (dc, ch 1, dc) in ch-1 sp, dc in next 4 dc: 9 dc.

Row 5: Ch 3, turn; dc in next 4 dc, ch 1, dc in ch-1 sp, dc in next 4 dc: 10 dc.

Row 6: Ch 3, turn; dc in next 4 dc, (dc, ch 1, dc) in ch-1 sp, dc in next 5 dc: 12 dc.

Row 7: Ch 3, turn; dc in next 5 dc and in ch-1 sp, ch 1, dc in next 6 dc: 13 dc.

Row 8: Ch 3, turn; dc in next 5 dc, (dc, ch 1, dc) in ch-1 sp, dc in next 7 dc: 15 dc.

Row 9: Ch 3, turn; dc in next 7 dc, ch 1, dc in ch-1 sp, dc in next 7 dc: 16 dc.

Row 10: Ch 3, turn; dc in next 7 dc, (dc, ch 1, dc) in ch-1 sp, dc in next 8 dc: 18 dc.

Row 11: Ch 3, turn; dc in next 8 dc and in ch-1 sp, ch 1, dc in next 9 dc: 19 dc.

Row 12: Ch 3, turn; dc in next 8 dc, (dc, ch 1, dc) in ch-1 sp, dc in next 10 dc: 21 dc.

Row 13: Ch 3, turn; dc in next 10 dc, ch 1, dc in ch-1 sp, dc in next 10 dc; do not fasten off.

Note: You will need 8 ea of Granny Blocks 3 and 4. Make 4 Block 3/Wedge/Block 3 units and 4 Block 4/Wedge/Block 4 units.

Assembly

Step 1: With ws tog, sc in any corner ch-2 sp of Block, * (ch 3, working in ends of Wedge rows, sk next row, sc around last dc on next row of Wedge, sc in next ch-sp on Block) twice, ch 2, sc around last dc on next row of Wedge, sc in next ch-sp on Block; rep from * once, ch 3, sk next row of Wedge, sc around last dc on next row of Wedge, sc in next ch-sp on Block, ch 1, sc in beg ring of Wedge, sk next dc of Block, sc in next dc of Block, ch 1, sc in corner ch-2 sp of Block, sc in corner ch-2 sp of next Block, ch 1, sk next dc of Block, sc in next dc of Block, sc in beg ring of Wedge, ch 1, sc in next ch-sp of Block, sc around last dc on next row of Wedge, ch 3, sc in next ch-sp of Block, sk next row of Wedge, sc around last dc on next row of Wedge, ch 2, sc in next ch-sp of Block, sc around last dc on next row of Wedge, (ch 3, sc in next ch-sp of Block, sk next row of Wedge, sc around last dc on next row of Wedge) twice, ch 2, sc in next ch-sp of Block, sc around last dc on next row of Wedge, ch 3, sc in next ch-sp of Block, sk next row of Wedge, sc around last dc on next row of Wedge, ch 3, sc in next ch-sp of Block; join with sl st to top of beg ch-3 of Wedge; fasten off.

Note: Pin Wedge units to Star, alternating colors and aligning corner ch-2 sps of Blocks with Point ch-2 sps of Stars. Center ch-1 sp of

ea Wedge should align with center dc of ea Star side.

Step 2: Join B in any Point ch-2 sp with sl st, ch 1, sc in corner ch-2 sp of Block, * (ch 3, sc in next ch-sp of Block, sc in next ch-sp of Star) 7 times, (ch 3, sk next 3 dc of Wedge, sc in next dc of Wedge, sc in next ch-sp of Star) twice, ch 2, sc in next ch-1 sp of Wedge, sk next dc of Star, sc in next dc of Star, ch 2, sk next dc of Wedge, sc in next dc of Wedge, sc in next ch-sp of Star, (ch 3, sk next 3 dc of Wedge, sc in next dc of Wedge, sc in next ch-sp of Star) twice; rep from * 7 times; join with sl st to beg sc; do not fasten off.

Edging

Ch 1, sc in same sp, * work 28 sc evenly sp across to next corner ch-2 sp, 3 sc in corner ch-2 sp, work 28 sc evenly sp across to next corner ch-2 sp, sc in same ch-2 sp, sc in joining, sc in next ch-2 sp; rep from * around; join with sl st to beg sc; fasten off.

Half Granny Block (Make 4.)
Note: To change colors, work last yo of prev st with new color.
With C, ch 4, join with sl st to form ring.

Row 1 (ws): Ch 4, (cl, ch 2, cl, ch 1, dc) in ring.

Row 2 (rs): Ch 4, turn; cl in next ch-1 sp, ch 1, (cl, ch 2, cl) in next ch-2 sp, ch 1, cl in next ch-1 sp, ch 1, dc in 3rd ch of beg ch-4, change to MC; fasten off C.

Row 3: With MC, ch 4, turn; (cl in next ch-1 sp, ch 1) twice, (cl, ch 2, cl) in ch-2 sp, ch 1, cl in next ch-1 sp, ch 1, cl in next ch-1 sp, ch 1, dc in 3rd ch of beg ch-4.

Row 4: Ch 4, turn; (cl in next ch-1 sp, ch 1) 3 times, (cl, ch 2, cl) in ch-2 sp, ch 1, (cl in next ch-1 sp, ch 1) twice, cl in next ch-1 sp, ch 1, cl in next ch-1 sp, ch 1, dc in 3rd ch of beg ch-4, change to A; fasten off MC.

Row 5: With A, ch 4, turn; (cl in next ch-1 sp, ch 1) 4 times, (cl, ch 2, cl) in ch-2 sp, ch 1, (cl in next ch-1 sp, ch 1) 3 times, cl in next ch-1 sp, ch 1, cl in next ch-1 sp, ch 1, dc in 3rd ch of beg ch-4.

Row 6: Ch 4, turn; (cl in next ch-1 sp, ch 1) 5 times, (cl, ch 2, cl) in ch-2 sp, ch 1, (cl in next ch-1 sp, ch 1) 4 times, cl in next ch-1 sp, ch 1, cl in next ch-1 sp, ch 1, dc in 3rd ch of beg ch-4; fasten off A.

Assembly

Referring to **Assembly Diagram,** join 1 Half Granny Block to ea side of Star as folls: With rs of Half Granny Block facing and point at top, join B in bottom right corner ch-4 sp with sl st, ch 4, sc in corner sc of Block, (cl in next ch-1 sp of Half Block, sk next 3 sc of Block, sc in next sc of Block) 6 times, cl in top ch-2 sp of Half Block, sc in Star point, cl in top ch-2 sp of Half Block, sk next 3 sc of next Block, sc in next sc of Block, (cl in next ch-1 sp of Half Block, sk next 3 sc of Block, sc in next sc of Block) 6 times, ch 1, dc in 3rd ch of ch-4 of Half Block; fasten off.

Corner Border

Note: You will need 1 Granny Block 1 for ea corner.

Row 1 (rs): With rs facing, join B in sc 2 sts before any Wedge tip with sl st, ch 1, sc in same sc, ch 1, sk next 2 sc, * (dc in next 3 sc, ch 1, sk next sc) 7 times, (cl, ch 2, cl) in next sc, (ch 1, sk next sc, dc in next 3 sc) 6 times **, sk next 2 sc, tr in next sc [joining], sk next 2 sc; rep from * to ** once, ch 1, sk next sc, dc in next 3 sc, ch 1, sk next 2 sc, sl st in next 2 sc.

Row 2 (ws): Ch 1, turn; cl in first ch-1 sp, * (ch 1, cl in next ch-1 sp) across to next ch-2 sp, ch 1, (cl, ch 2, cl) in ch-2 sp **, (ch 1, cl in next ch-1 sp) across to tr, tr in tr, cl in next ch-1 sp; rep from * to ** once, (ch 1, cl in next ch-1 sp) across, ch 1, sk 2 sc, sl st in next 2 sc.

Assembly Diagram

Rows 3 and 4: Rep row 2 twice, change to MC at end of last row; fasten off B.

Rows 5–7: With MC, rep row 2, 3 times, change to C at end of last row; fasten off MC.

Rows 8 and 9: With C, rep row 2 twice; do not fasten off.

Row 10 [Assembly]: Ch 1, turn; cl in first ch-1 sp, (ch 1, cl in next ch-1 sp) across to next ch-2 sp, cl in ch 2 sp, sc in corner ch-2 sp of Granny Block, cl in same corner ch-2 sp of Afghan, (sc in next ch-sp of Block, cl in next ch-sp of Afghan) across to next corner ch-2 sp of Block, sc in corner ch-2 sp of Block, tr in tr of Afghan, sc in same corner ch-2 sp of Block, (cl in next ch-sp of Afghan, sc in next ch-sp of Block) across to next corner ch-2 sp of Afghan, cl in ch-2 sp, sc in corner ch-2 sp of Granny Block, cl in same corner ch-2 sp of Afghan, (cl in next ch-1 sp of Afghan, ch 1) across, ch 1, sk 2 sc, sl st in next sc; do not fasten off.

Rep rows 1–10 for ea rem corner.

Edging

Dc in corner sc, * (3 sc around next dc, 2 dc around next dc) 7 times, 3 sc around next dc, dc in next dc, cl in next ch-sp and in ea ch-sp across to next corner, 7 dc in corner, cl in next ch-sp and in ea ch-sp across to next Half Granny Block; rep from * around; join with sl st to top of beg dc; fasten off.

Afghan by Kathy Blakely
Ririe, Idaho

Pinwheel

Create the intricate-looking swirls in this gorgeous afghan with one simple motif. Once you make the flower centers, the rest is just single crochet and chain stitches.

Materials

Worsted-weight acrylic yarn, approximately:
56 oz. (3,165 yd.) burgundy
Size I crochet hook or size to obtain gauge
Yarn needle

Finished Size

Approximately 52½" x 79"

Gauge

Ea motif = 8¾"

Pattern Stitches

Beg tr-cl: Ch 4, [Yo twice, insert hook in st indicated, yo and pull up lp, (yo and pull through 2 lps) twice] twice, yo and pull through all 4 lps on hook.

Tr-cl: [Yo twice, insert hook in st indicated, yo and pull up lp, (yo and pull through 2 lps) twice] 3 times, yo and pull through all 4 lps on hook.

Pinwheel (Make 61.)

Ch 2.

Rnd 1 (rs): 6 sc in 2nd sc from hook; join with sl st to beg sc.

Rnd 2: Beg tr-cl in joining, (ch 4, tr-cl in next sc) 5 times, ch 4; join with sl st to top of beg tr-cl.

Note: Do not join rem rnds. Mark beg ch-4 sp of ea rnd.

Rnd 3: * Ch 4, 2 sc in next ch-4 sp **, sc in top of next tr-cl; rep from * 4 times, then rep from * to ** once, sc in joining: 18 sc.

Rnd 4: * Ch 4, 2 sc in next ch-4 sp, sc in next 2 sc, sk next sc; rep from * 5 times: 24 sc.

Rnd 5: * Ch 4, 2 sc in next ch-4 sp, sc in next 3 sc, sk next sc; rep from * 5 times: 30 sc.

Rnd 6: * Ch 4, 2 sc in next ch-4 sp, sc in next 4 sc, sk next sc; rep from * 5 times: 36 sc.

Rnd 7: * Ch 4, 2 sc in next ch-4 sp, sc in next 5 sc, sk next sc; rep from * 5 times: 42 sc.

Rnd 8: * Ch 4, 2 sc in next ch-4 sp, sc in next 6 sc, sk next sc; rep from * 5 times: 48 sc.

Rnd 9: * Ch 4, 2 sc in next ch-4 sp, sc in next 7 sc, sk next sc; rep from * 5 times: 54 sc.

Rnd 10: * Ch 4, 2 sc in next ch-4 sp, sc in next 8 sc, sk next sc; rep from * 5 times: 60 sc.

Rnd 11: * Ch 4, 2 sc in next ch-4 sp, sc in next 9 sc, sk next sc; rep from * 5 times: 66 sc.

Rnd 12: * Ch 4, 2 sc in next ch-4 sp, sc in next 10 sc, sk next sc; rep from * 5 times; join with sl st to last sc of rnd 11; fasten off: 72 sc.

Assembly

Join 2 Pinwheels tog as folls: With rs facing, beg whipstitch in any ch-4 sp, and work across to next ch-4 sp; fasten off. Join 6 Pinwheels tog to form 1 Strip A. Rep to form 6 Strip As. Join 5 Pinwheels tog to form 1 Strip B. Rep to form 5 Strip Bs. Beg and ending with Strip A, alternate strips and whipstitch tog.

Border

With rs facing, join yarn in any sc with sl st, ch 1, * working from left to right, sc in ea sc across to next ch-4 sp, 4 sc in ch-4 sp; rep from * around; join with sl st to beg sc; fasten off.

Afghan by Carla Kisielnicki
McKeesport, Pennsylvania

Memory Star

Combine solid and bicolored granny squares for a memorable spread. Once you know how to make triangles and squares, you can experiment with lots of traditional quilt patterns

Materials

Worsted-weight acrylic yarn, approximately:
32 oz. (1,760 yd.) white, MC
24 oz. (1,320 yd.) light gray, A
32 oz. (1,760 yd.) raspberry, B
24 oz. (1,320 yd.) mint, C
Size J crochet hook or size to obtain gauge

Finished Size

Approximately 76" x 76"

Gauge

Ea square = 3¾"

Note: To change colors, pick up new color, yo and pull through lp on hook [color change ch made]. Do not carry yarn not in use.

Solid Square (Make 84 with MC, 16 with A, 20 with B, and 64 with C.)

Ch 6, join with sl st to form ring.
Rnd 1 (rs): Ch 3 [counts as first dc throughout], 2 dc in ring, ch 2, (3 dc in ring, ch 2) 3 times; join with sl st to top of beg ch-3.
Rnd 2: Sl st in next 2 dc and in next ch-2 sp, ch 3, (2 dc, ch 2, 3 dc) in same sp, * ch 1, (3 dc, ch 2, 3 dc) in next ch-2 sp; rep from * twice more, ch 1; join with sl st to top of beg ch-3.
Rnd 3: Sl st in next 2 dc and in next ch-2 sp, ch 3, (2 dc, ch 2, 3 dc) in same sp, * ch 1, 3 dc in next ch-1 sp, ch 1, (3 dc, ch 2, 3 dc) in next ch-2 sp; rep from * twice more, ch 1, 3 dc in next ch-1 sp, ch 1; join with sl st to top of beg ch-3; fasten off.

Triangle Square (Make 40 with MC and B, 32 with MC and C, 108 with A and B, and 36 with B and C.)

With first color, ch 6, join with sl st to form ring.
Rnd 1 (rs): Ch 3, (2 dc, ch 2, 3 dc) in ring, ch 1, change colors [color change ch made], (3 dc in ring, ch 2) twice; join with sl st to top of beg ch-3.
Rnd 2 (ws): Turn; sl st in same ch-2 sp, ch 3, 2 dc in same sp, ch 1, (3 dc, ch 2, 3 dc) in next ch-2 sp, ch 1, 3 dc in next ch-2 sp, ch 1, change colors [color change ch made], 3 dc in same ch-2 sp, ch 1, (3 dc, ch 2, 3 dc) in next ch-2 sp, ch 1, 3 dc in next ch-2 sp, ch 2; join with sl st to top of beg ch-3.
Rnd 3 (rs): Turn; sl st in same ch-2 sp, ch 3, 2 dc in same sp, ch 1, 3 dc in next ch-1 sp, ch 1, (3 dc, ch 2, 3 dc) in next ch-2 sp, ch 1, 3 dc in next ch-1 sp, ch 1, 3 dc in next ch-2 sp, ch 1, change colors [color change ch made], 3 dc in same ch-2 sp, ch 1, 3 dc in next ch-1 sp, (3 dc, ch 2, 3 dc) in next ch-2 sp, ch 1, 3 dc in next ch-1 sp, ch 1, 3 dc in next ch-2 sp, ch 2; join

(continued)

Assembly Diagram

with sl st to top of beg ch-3; fasten off.

Assembly

With rs tog and referring to ***Assembly Diagram,*** sl st squares tog through ft lps only.

Border

With rs facing, join A in any corner with sl st, ch 3, 7 dc same sp, sl st in next ch-1 sp, (6 dc in next ch-1 sp, sl st in next ch-1 sp) across to next corner ch-2 sp, * 8 dc in corner sp, sl st in next ch-1 sp, (6 dc in next ch-1 sp, sl st in next ch-1 sp) across to next corner ch-2 sp; rep from * around; join with sl st to top of beg ch-3; fasten off.

Afghan by Linda Laney
Coos Bay, Oregon

Textured Sampler

Showcase seven stitch patterns with this
handsome striped afghan.

Materials

Sportweight acrylic yarn,
approximately:
32½ oz. (3,250 yd.) cream, MC
25 oz. (2,500 yd.) tan, A
25 oz. (2,500 yd.) blue, B
Size G crochet hook or size to
obtain gauge

Finished Size

Approximately 57" x 74", without
fringe

Gauge

In first pat, 12 sts and 14 rows = 3"

Pattern Stitches

Cl: (Yo, insert hook in st indicated,
yo and pull up lp, yo and pull
through 2 lps) 5 times, yo and pull
through all 6 lps on hook, ch 1.
FPdc: Yo, insert hook from front to
back around st indicated, yo and pull
up lp, (yo and pull through 2 lps)
twice.
BPdc: Yo, insert hook from back to
front around st indicated, yo and
pull up lp, (yo and pull through 2
lps) twice.
Shell: 5 dc in st indicated.
Half Shell: 3 dc in st indicated.
Pocket st: Working from front to
back, (sc, hdc, dc) around st
indicated.

Note: Afghan is worked sideways.

With A, ch 289.
Row 1 (rs): Sl st in 3rd ch from
hook, (hdc in next ch, sl st in next
ch) across: 288 sts.
Rows 2–14: Ch 2 [counts as first
hdc throughout], turn; (sl st in next
hdc, hdc in next sl st) across to beg
ch-2, sl st in top of beg ch-2; fasten
off after last row: 288 sts.
Row 15: With rs facing, join B in
top right corner with sl st, ch 1, sc in
same st and in ea st across: 288 sc.
Rows 16–18: Ch 1, turn; sc in same
sc and in ea sc across: 288 sc.

Row 19: Ch 1, turn; sc in first 5 sc,
(cl in next sc, sc in next 5 sc) across
to last 6 sc, sc in last 6 sc: 47 cls.
Row 20: Ch 1, turn; sc in ea sc and
ea cl across: 288 sc.
Rows 21–23: Rep row 16, 3 times;
fasten off.
Row 24: With rs facing, join A in
top right corner with sl st, ch 2
[counts as first hdc], (sl st in next st,
hdc in next st) across to last st,
sl st in last sc: 288 sts.
Rows 25–37: Rep row 2, 13 times;
fasten off after last row.
Row 38: With rs facing, join MC in
top right corner with sl st, ch 3
[counts as first dc throughout], dc in
next st and in ea st across: 288 dc.
Rows 39–41: Ch 3, turn; FPdc
around next 5 dc, * BPdc around
next 6 dc, FPdc around next 6 dc;
rep from * across to last 6 dc,
BPdc around next 5 dc, dc in top of
beg ch-3.
Rows 42–44: Ch 3, turn; BPdc
around next 5 dc, * FPdc around
next 6 dc, BPdc around next 6 dc;
rep from * across to last 6 dc,
FPdc around next 5 dc, dc in top of
beg ch-3.
Rows 45–56: Rep rows 39–44
twice; fasten off after last row.
Row 57: With rs facing, join A in
top right corner with sl st, ch 3,
2 dc in same st [beg half shell
made], * sk 2 dc, sc in next dc,
sk 2 dc, shell in next dc; rep from *
across to last 5 dc, sk 2 dc, sc in next
dc, sk 1 dc, half shell in top of beg
ch-3: 46 shells and 2 half shells.
Row 58: Ch 1, turn; sc in first dc,
* shell in next sc, sc in top of next
shell [center dc]; rep from * across
to last sc, shell in last sc, sc in top of
beg ch-3: 48 shells.
Row 59: Ch 3, 2 dc in same st,
* sc in top of next shell, shell in next
sc; rep from * across to last shell,
sc in top of last shell, half shell in
top of beg sc.
Rows 60–70: Rep rows 58 and 59
alternately, 5 times, then rep row 58
once.

Row 71: Ch 3, turn; * hdc in next
2 dc, sc in next dc, hdc in next 2 dc,
dc in next sc; rep from * across to
last shell, hdc in next 2 dc, sc in next
dc, hdc in next dc, sk next dc, dc in
last sc; fasten off: 288 sts.
Row 72: With rs facing, join MC in
top right corner with sl st, ch 3,
dc in next st and in ea st across:
288 dc.
Row 73: Ch 3, turn; FPdc around
next 2 dc, * BPdc around next 3 dc,
FPdc around next 3 dc; rep from *
across to last 3 dc, BPdc around next
2 dc, dc in top of beg ch-3.
Row 74: Ch 3, turn; BPdc around
next 2 dc, * FPdc around next 3 dc,
BPdc around next 3 dc; rep from *
across to last 3 dc, FPdc around next
2 dc, dc in top of beg ch-3.
Rows 75–86: Rep rows 73 and 74
alternately, 6 times; fasten off after
last row.
Row 87 (ws): With ws facing, join A
in top right corner with sl st, ch 3,
dc in next st and in ea st across:
288 sts.
Row 88: Turn; sl st in first dc,
* pocket st around same dc, sk 2 dc,
sl st in next dc; rep from * across to
last 3 dc, pocket st around same dc,
sk 1 dc, sl st in top of beg ch-3:
96 pocket sts.
Row 89: Ch 3, turn; working behind
last row, dc in ea dc 2 rows below:
288 dc.
Rows 90–93: Rep rows 88 and 89
alternately, twice; fasten off after last
row.
Row 94: With rs facing, join B in
top right corner with sl st, ch 1, sc in
same st and in ea st across: 288 sc.
Rows 95–97: Ch 1, turn; sc in same
sc and in ea sc across: 288 sc.
Row 98: Ch 1, turn; sc in first 5 sc,
(cl in next sc, sc in next 5 sc) across
to last 6 sc, sc in last 6 sc: 47 cls.
Row 99: Ch 1, turn; sc in ea sc and
ea cl across: 288 sc.
Row 100: Ch 1, turn; sc in first 2 sc,
(cl in next sc, sc in next 5 sc) across
to last 3 sc, sc in last 3 sc:
48 cls.

Row 101: Rep row 99.

Rows 102 and 103: Rep rows 98 and 99 once.

Rows 104–106: Rep row 95, 3 times; fasten off after last row.

Rows 107–113: Rep rows 87–93 once.

Rows 114–128: Rep rows 72–86 once.

Rows 129–143: Rep rows 57–71 once.

Rows 144–162: Rep rows 38–56 once.

Rows 163–176: Rep rows 24–37 once.

Rows 177–185: Rep rows 15–23 once.

Rows 186–199: Rep rows 24–37 once.

Edging

Row 1 (rs): With rs facing, join B in top left corner with sl st, work 184 sc evenly sp across ends of rows.

Rows 2 and 3: Ch 1, turn; sc in first sc and in ea sc across: 184 sc.

Row 4: Ch 1, turn; sc in in first sc, * ch 3, sk next 2 sc, sc in next sc; rep from * across; fasten off: 46 ch-3 sps.

Row 5 (rs): With rs facing, join B in bottom right corner with sl st, work 184 sc evenly sp across ends of rows.

Rows 6–8: Rep rows 2–4 once.

Fringe

For ea tassel, referring to page 159 of General Directions, cut 7 (16") lengths of B. Working across short ends, knot 1 tassel in every other ch-3 sp.

Afghan by Monica Baty
Gainesville, Florida

29

Pink Diamonds

Learn easy increases and decreases in single crochet with this pretty pattern. For a whimsical look, change the colors to harlequin red and gold.

Materials

Worsted-weight acrylic yarn, approximately:
56 oz. (3,165 yd.) white, MC
32 oz. (1,810 yd.) rose, A
24 oz. (1,360 yd.) pink, B
Size J crochet hook or size to obtain gauge
Yarn needle

Finished Size
Approximately 71" x 87"

Gauge
10 sc and 11 rows = 3"

Pattern Stitches

Inc: 2 sc in st indicated.
Dec: (Insert hook in next st, yo and pull up lp) twice, yo and pull through all 3 lps on hook [counts as 1 sc].

Note: To change colors, work last yo of prev st with new color, dropping prev color to ws of work. Do not carry yarn across row.

Diamond Strip A (Make 17.)
With A, ch 2.
Row 1 (rs): Sc in 2nd ch from hook.
Row 2: Ch 1, turn; 3 sc in sc.
Row 3: Ch 1, turn; sc in first sc and in ea sc across: 3 sc.
Row 4: Ch 1, turn; inc in first sc, sc in ea sc across to last sc, inc in last sc: 5 sc.
Row 5: Ch 1, turn; sc in first sc and in ea sc across: 5 sc.
Rows 6–13: Rep rows 4 and 5 alternately, 4 times: 13 sc in last row.

Row 14: Ch 1, turn; dec in first 2 sc, sc in ea sc across to last 2 sc, dec in last 2 sc: 11 sc.
Row 15: Ch 1, turn; sc in first sc and in ea sc across: 11 sc.
Rows 16–23: Rep rows 14 and 15 alternately, 4 times: 3 sc in last row.
Row 24: Ch 1, turn; dec in first 2 sc, change to B: 1 sc.
Row 25: Ch 1, turn; sc in sc: 1 sc.
Rows 26–47: Rep rows 2–23 once.
Row 48: Ch 1, turn; dec in first 2 sc, change to A: 1 sc.
Row 49: Rep row 25.
Rows 50–311: Rep rows 2–49, 5 times, then rep rows 2–23 once.
Row 312: Ch 1, turn; dec in first 2 sc; fasten off: 1 sc.

Diamond Strip B (Make 16.)
With MC, ch 14.
Row 1 (rs): Sc in 2nd ch from hook and in ea ch across: 13 sc.

Row 2: Ch 1, turn; sc in first sc and in ea sc across: 13 sc.
Row 3: Ch 1, turn; dec in first 2 sc, sc in ea sc across to last 2 sc, dec in last 2 sc: 11 sc.
Row 4: Ch 1, turn; sc in first sc and in ea sc across: 11 sc.
Rows 5–12: Rep rows 3 and 4 alternately, 4 times: 3 sc in last row.
Row 13: Ch 1, turn; dec in first 2 sc: 1 sc.
Row 14: Ch 1, turn; sc in sc: 1 sc.
Row 15: Ch 1, turn; 3 sc in sc.
Row 16: Ch 1, turn; sc in first sc and in ea sc across: 3 sc.
Row 17: Ch 1, turn; inc in first sc, sc in ea sc across to last sc, inc in last sc: 5 sc.
Row 18: Ch 1, turn; sc in first sc and in ea sc across: 5 sc.
Rows 19–26: Rep rows 17 and 18 alternately, 4 times: 13 sc in last row.
Rows 27–314: Rep rows 3–26, 12 times; fasten off.

Assembly
Referring to photo, beg and ending with Strip A, alternate strips and whipstitch tog.

Border
With rs facing, join MC in any corner with sl st, ch 1, 3 sc in same st, sc evenly across to next corner, * 3 sc in corner, sc evenly across to next corner; rep from * around; join with sl st to beg sc; fasten off.

Afghan by Louise Allbro
Barre, Massachusetts

Bluebirds and Bluebells

This charted afghan-stitch design is accented with textured bands of blue.

Materials

Worsted-weight acrylic yarn, approximately:

- 40 oz. (2,260 yd.) cream, MC
- 10½ oz. (595 yd.) light blue, A
- 16 oz. (905 yd.) medium blue, B
- 1½ oz. (85 yd.) dark blue, C
- 1¾ oz. (100 yd.) bright blue, D
- 2 yd. black, E
- 1½ oz. (85 yd.) white, F
- 1½ oz. (85 yd.) gray, G
- 3½ oz. (200 yd.) sage green, H
- 1¾ oz. (100 yd.) rust, I
- Size H afghan hook or size to obtain gauge
- Size H crochet hook or size to obtain gauge
- Yarn needle

Finished Size

Approximately 46" x 60", without fringe

Gauge

In afghan st, 16 sts and 13 rows = 4"
In bead st, 13 sts and 14 rows = 4"

Pattern Stitch

Bead st: Insert hook in st indicated, yo and pull up lp, (holding back last lp on hook, yo and pull through first lp on hook only) 3 times, yo and pull through both lps on hook.

Bead St Panel (Make 4.)

With crochet hook and MC, ch 196.
Note: Panel is worked vertically with rs facing throughout. To join yarn with sc, beg with sl st on hook, insert hook in st indicated, yo and pull up lp, yo and pull through both lps on hook.
Row 1 (rs): Sc in 2nd ch from hook and in ea ch across; fasten off: 195 sc.

Row 2 (rs): Join MC in first sc of prev row with sc, (bead st in next st, sc in next st) across; fasten off: 195 sts.
Row 3: Join MC in first sc of prev row with sc, (sc in next st, bead st in next st) across; fasten off: 195 sts.
Rows 4–16: Rep rows 2 and 3 alternately, using foll color sequence: 2 rows A, 3 rows B, 1 row MC, 3 rows B, 2 rows A, 2 rows MC.

Left Panel

Note: See page 148 for afghan st directions. To change colors in afghan st: **Step 1:** drop yarn to ws of work, insert hook under next vertical bar and pull up lp with new color. Do not carry yarn over more than 3 sts. **Step 2:** Yo and pull through 2 lps on hook until 1 lp of current color rem on hook, drop yarn to ws of work, pick up new color, yo and pull through 2 lps on hook.
With afghan hook and MC, ch 21.
Rows 1–6: Work 6 rows of afghan st: 21 sts.
Rows 7–72: Foll **Left Panel Chart** on page 36: 21 sts.
Rows 73–190: Rep rows 7–72 once, then rep rows 7–58 once.
Rows 191–195: With MC, work 5 rows of afghan st: 21 sts.

Row 196: Sl st in ea vertical bar across; fasten off.

Right Panel

With afghan hook and MC, ch 21.
Rows 1–6: Work 6 rows of afghan st: 21 sts.
Rows 7–72: Foll **Right Panel Chart** on page 36: 21 sts.
Rows 73–190: Rep rows 7–72 once, then rep rows 7–58 once.
Rows 191–195: With MC, work 5 rows of afghan st: 21 sts.
Row 196: Sl st in ea vertical bar across; fasten off.

Bird Panel

With afghan hook and MC, ch 65.
Rows 1–5: Work 5 rows of afghan st: 65 sts.
Row 6: Foll **Bird Panel Chart** on pages 34 and 35: 65 sts.
Rows 7–195: Cont foll **Bird Panel Chart** as est.
Row 196: Sl st in ea vertical bar across; fasten off.
Embroidery
Referring to page 159 of General Directions and **Bird Panel Chart,** straightstitch beaks and make French knot eyes with E.

(continued on page 36)

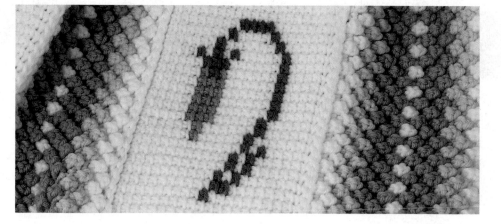

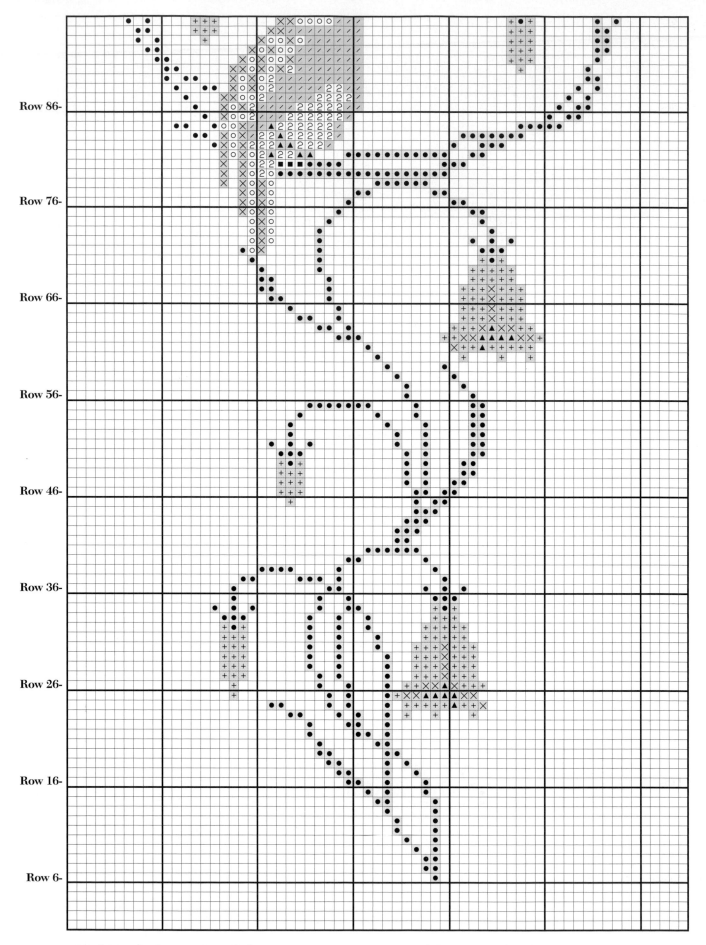

Row 86-

Row 76-

Row 66-

Row 56-

Row 46-

Row 36-

Row 26-

Row 16-

Row 6-

Bird Panel Chart —Top of chart is on page 35. Bottom of chart is on this page. Key is on page 36.

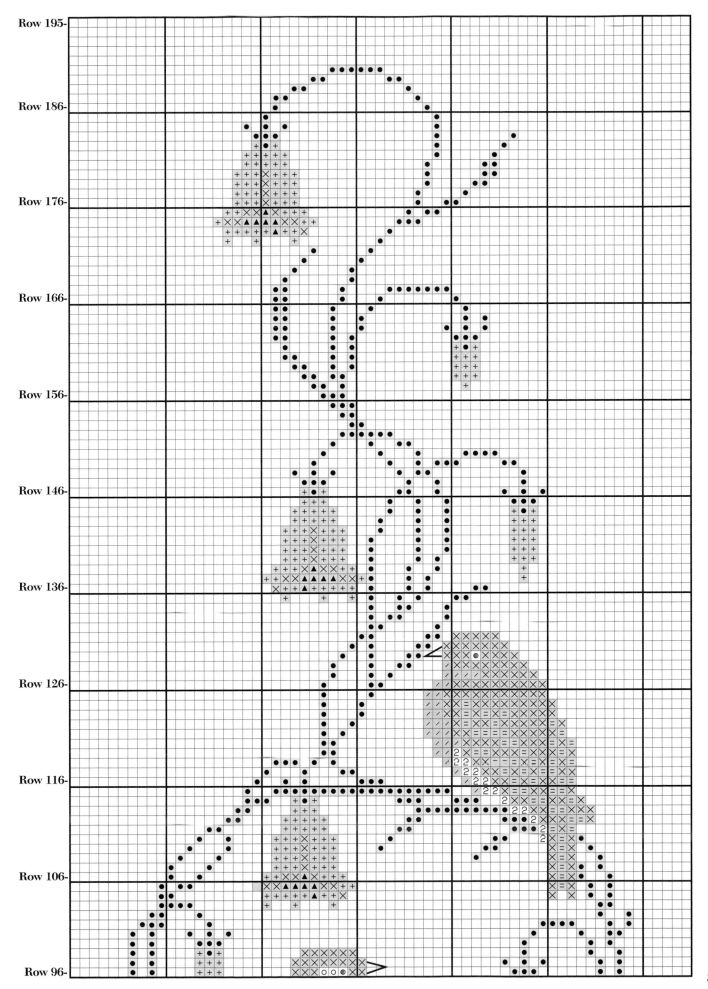

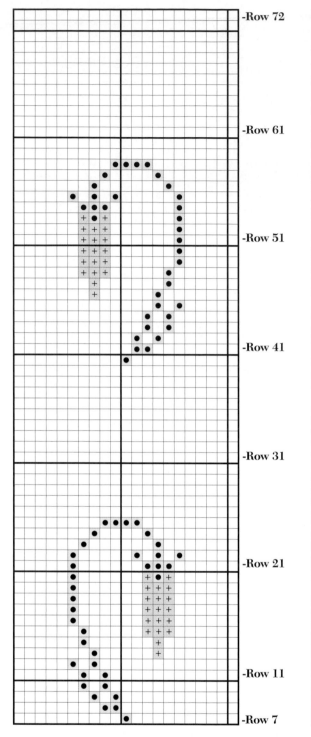

Left Panel Chart

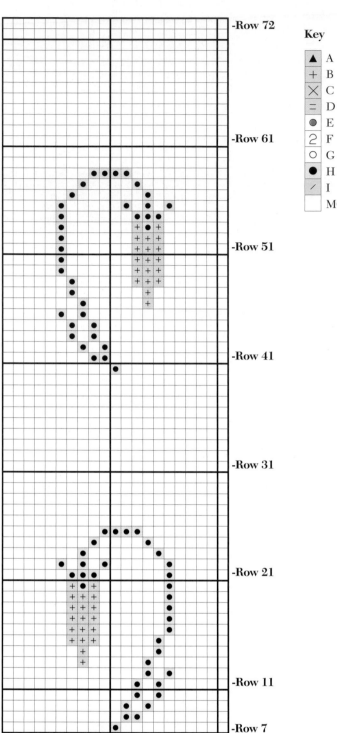

Right Panel Chart

Key

▲	A
+	B
✕	C
=	D
●	E (French knot)
2	F
○	G
●	H
/	I
	MC

Assembly

With crochet hook, ws tog and working in ft lps only, sl st panels tog in foll sequence: Bead Panel, Left Panel, Bead Panel, Bird Panel, Bead Panel, Right Panel, Bead Panel.

Border

With rs facing and crochet hook, join MC in top right corner with sl st, ch 1, 3 sc in same st, sc in ea st across to next corner, * 3 sc in corner, sc evenly across to next corner; rep from * around; join with sl st to beg sc; fasten off.

Fringe

For ea tassel, referring to page 159 of General Directions, cut 5 (16") lengths of yarn. Working across short ends and matching colors, knot 1 tassel in approximately every other st.

Afghan by Dorothy Warrell
Granville, Ohio

Floral Fantasy

Get the delicate look of spring and the warmth needed for winter in one afghan. Work the tiny blooms in sportweight yarn and then switch to worsted-weight yarn to finish the blocks.

Materials 🧶🧶

Worsted-weight acrylic yarn, approximately:
40 oz. (2,260 yd.) white, MC
7 oz. (400 yd.) berry, A
12 oz. (700 yd.) rose-and-gray multicolored, B
Sportweight acrylic yarn, approximately:
12½ oz. (1,250 yd.) light pink, C
5 oz. (500 yd.) light green, D
Sizes E, F, and G crochet hooks or sizes to obtain gauge

Finished Size
Approximately 47" x 58"

Gauge
Flower = 2½"
Four-Flower Block = 10¾"

Pattern Stitches
BPsc: Insert hook from back to front around post of st indicated, yo and pull up lp, yo and pull through 2 lps on hook.
Dtr: Yo 3 times, insert hook in st indicated, yo and pull up lp, (yo and pull through 2 lps on hook) 4 times.

Flower 1 (Make 40.)
With small hook and C, ch 4, join with sl st to form ring.
Rnd 1 (rs): Ch 2 [counts as first hdc], 11 hdc in ring; join with sl st to top of beg ch-2: 12 hdc.
Rnd 2: Ch 1, BPsc around next hdc, * ch 3, sk next hdc, BPsc around next hdc; rep from * 4 times more, ch 3; join with sl st to beg BPsc: 6 ch-3 sps.
Rnd 3: (Sl st, ch 3, 11 dc, ch 3, sl st) in next ch-3 sp and in ea ch-3 sp around; join with sl st to beg sl st: 6 petals.
Rnd 4: Ch 1, BPsc around next dc, * ch 3, BPsc around first dc of next petal; rep from * around, ch 3; join with sl st to beg BPsc; fasten off.

Flower 2 (Make 40.)
Rnds 1–3: Work as for Flower 1

through rnd 3.
Rnd 4: Ch 1, BPsc around next dc, * ch 3, BPsc around first dc of next petal; rep from * 4 times more, ch 1, sc in 2nd ch of any ch-3 lp of Flower 1, ch 1; join with sl st to beg BPsc of Flower 2; fasten off.

Two-Flower Block (Make 40.)
Note: Change to medium hook.
Rnd 1 (rs): With rs facing, join D to Flower 2 in 3rd ch-3 sp from joining with sl st, ch 6 [counts as first dc plus ch 3], * (tr, ch 5, tr) in next BPsc, ch 2, dc in next BPsc, ch 2, tr in next BPsc, ch 2, (dtr, ch 2, dtr) in joining, ch 2, tr in next BPsc, ch 2, dc in next BPsc, ch 2, (tr, ch 5, tr) in next BPsc, ch 3 **, dc in next ch-3 sp, ch 3; rep from * to ** once; join with sl st to 3rd ch of beg ch-6; fasten off.
Note: Change to large hook.
Rnd 2: With rs facing, join MC in top right corner ch-5 sp with sl st, ch 3 [counts as first dc throughout], (dc, ch 3, 2 dc) in same sp, * dc in ea st and sp across to next corner ch-5 sp , (2 dc, ch 3, 2 dc) in corner ch-5 sp, (dc in next st, 2 dc in next sp) twice, (dc in next st, dc in next sp) 3 times, (dc in next st, 2 dc in next sp) twice, dc in next st **, (2 dc, ch 3, 2 dc) in corner ch-5 sp; rep from * to ** once; join with sl st to top of beg ch-3: 64 dc.
Rnd 3: Ch 3, dc in next dc, * (2 dc, ch 3, 2 dc) in corner ch-3 sp, dc in next dc and in ea dc across to next corner ch-3 sp; rep from * around; join with sl st to top of beg ch-3; fasten off: 80 dc.

Four-Flower Block (Make 20.)
Join Two-Flower Blocks as folls: With large hook, rs tog and working through bk lps only, join MC in corner ch-3 sp with sl st, ch 1, sc in same sp, sc in ea sc across to next corner ch-3 sp, sc in corner ch-3 sp; fasten off.

Edging
Rnd 1 (rs): With large hook and rs facing, join A in any corner ch-3 sp with sl st, ch 1, (sc, ch 3, sc) in same corner ch-3 sp, work 27 sc evenly sp across to next corner ch-3 sp, * (sc, ch 3, sc) in corner ch-3 sp, work 27 sc evenly sp across to next corner ch-3 sp; rep from * around; join with sl st to beg sc; fasten off: 116 sc.
Rnd 2: With large hook and rs facing, join B in any corner ch-3 sp with sl st, ch 6 [counts as first dc plus ch 3 throughout], dc in same sp, dc in next sc and in ea sc across to next corner ch-3 sp, * (dc, ch 3, dc) in corner ch-3 sp, dc in next sc and in ea sc across to next corner ch-3 sp; rep from * around; join with sl st in 3rd ch of beg ch-6; fasten off: 124 dc.
Rnd 3: With large hook and rs facing, join A in any corner ch-3 sp with sl st, ch 1, (sc, ch 3, sc) in same corner ch-3 sp, sc in ea dc across to next corner ch-3 sp, * (sc, ch 3, sc) in corner ch-3 sp, sc in ea dc across to next corner ch-3 sp; rep from * around; join with sl st to beg sc; fasten off: 132 sc.
Rnd 4: With large hook and rs facing, join B in any corner ch-3 sp with sl st, ch 6, dc in same sp, (ch 1, sk next sc, dc in next sc) across to next corner ch-3 sp, * ch 1, (dc, ch 3, dc) in corner ch-3 sp, (ch 1, sk next sc, dc in next sc) across to next corner ch-3 sp; rep from * around, ch 1; join with sl st in 3rd ch of beg ch-6; fasten off: 72 dc.
Rnd 5: With large hook and rs facing, join C in any corner ch-3 sp with sl st, ch 1, sc in same sp, ch 1, dc in ch-3 sp 2 rnds below, sc in next dc, (dc in next sc 2 rnds below, sc in next dc) across to next corner ch-3 sp, * dc in ch-3 sp 2 rnds below, ch 1, sc in ch-3 sp, ch 1, dc in ch-3 sp 2 rnds below, sc in next dc, (dc in next sc 2 rnds below, sc in next dc) across to next corner ch-3 sp; rep from * around, dc in ch-3 sp 2 rnds below, ch 1; join with sl st to beg sc; fasten off: 76 dc.

Assembly

Afghan is 5 blocks long and 4 blocks wide. Referring to photo, turn every other block 90° to form checkerboard pattern.

With large hook and rs tog and working through bk lps only, join C in corner ch-3 sp with sl st, ch 1, sc in same sp, sc in ea sc across to next corner ch-3 sp, sc in corner ch-3 sp; fasten off.

Border

Rnd 1 (rs): With large hook and rs facing, join MC in any corner sc with sl st, ch 6 [counts as first dc plus ch 3 throughout], dc in same st and in ea st across to next corner sc, * (dc, ch 3, dc) in corner sc, dc in ea st across to next corner sc; rep from * around; join with sl st to 3rd ch of beg ch-6.

Rnd 2: Sl st in corner ch-3 sp, ch 6, dc in same ch-3 sp, dc in next dc and in ea dc across to next corner ch-3 sp, * (dc, ch 3, dc) in corner ch-3 sp, dc in ea st across to next corner ch-3 sp; rep from * around; join with sl st to 3rd ch of beg ch-6.

Rnd 3: Sl st in corner ch-3 sp, ch 6, dc in same ch-3 sp, (ch 1, sk next dc, dc in next dc) across to next corner ch-3 sp, ch 1, * (dc, ch 3, dc) in corner ch-3 sp, (ch 1, sk next dc, dc in next dc) across to next corner ch-3 sp; rep from * around; join with sl st to 3rd ch of beg ch-6; fasten off.

Rnd 4: With rs facing, join C in any corner ch-3 sp with sl st, ch 1, sc in same sp, ch 1, dc in ch-3 sp 2 rnds below, sc in next dc, (dc in next dc 2 rnds below, sc in next dc) across to next corner ch-3 sp, * dc in ch-3 sp 2 rnds below, ch 1, sc in ch-3 sp, ch 1, dc in ch-3 sp 2 rnds below, sc in next dc, (dc in next dc 2 rnds below, sc in next dc) across to next corner ch-3 sp; rep from * around, dc in ch-3 sp 2 rnds below, ch 1; join with sl st to beg sc.

Rnd 5: With rs facing and working from left to right, ch 1, sc in same st, * ch 1, sc in next st, hdc in next st; rep from * around; join with sl st to beg sc; fasten off.

Afghan by Sarah Karnes
Wyoming, Michigan

Mum's the Word

Surround clusters of red popcorn-stitch chrysanthemums
with deep green leaves for Christmas cheer or use
oranges and yellows for autumn splendor.

Materials
Worsted-weight acrylic yarn,
    approximately:
38½ oz. (2,350 yd.) ecru, MC
17½ oz. (1,065 yd.) red, A
10½ oz. (640 yd.) green, B
Size H crochet hook or size to
    obtain gauge
Yarn needle

Finished Size
Approximately 51" x 70"

Gauge
Ea Square = 9½"

Pattern Stitches
Beg popcorn: Ch 3, 3 dc in ring,
drop lp from hook, insert hook in
top of beg ch-3, pull dropped lp
through.
Popcorn: 4 dc in st or sp indicated,
drop lp from hook, insert hook in
first dc of 4-dc grp, pull dropped lp
through.
Cl: 3 dc in sp indicated.
V-st: (Dc, ch 1, dc) in st or sp
indicated.

Square (Make 35.)
With A, ch 4, join with sl st to form
ring.
Rnd 1 (rs): Beg popcorn, ch 3,
(popcorn, ch 3) 3 times in ring; join
with sl st to top of beg popcorn:
4 popcorns.
Rnd 2: Sl st in next ch-3 sp,
(beg popcorn, ch 3, popcorn) in
same ch-3 sp, ch 3, * (popcorn, ch 3,
popcorn) in next ch-3 sp, ch 3; rep
from * around; join with sl st to top
of beg popcorn: 8 popcorns.

Rnd 3: Rep rnd 2; fasten off:
16 popcorns.
Rnd 4: With rs facing, join B in any
ch-3 sp with sl st, ch 4 [counts as
first tr], (2 tr, ch 2, 3 tr) in same
ch-3 sp [corner made], (cl in next
ch-3 sp) 3 times, * (3 tr, ch 2, 3 tr) in
next ch-3 sp, (cl in next ch-3 sp) 3
times; rep from * around; join with
sl st to top of beg ch-4; fasten off.
Rnd 5: With rs facing, join MC in
any corner ch-2 sp with sl st, ch 4
[counts as first dc plus ch 1 through-
out], (dc, ch 2, V-st) in same corner
ch-2 sp, * sk next tr, V-st in next tr,
(V-st in center dc of next cl) 3 times,
sk next tr, V-st in next tr **, (V-st,
ch 2, V-st) in corner ch-2 sp; rep
from * around, ending last rep at **;
join with sl st to 3rd ch of beg ch-4:
28 V-sts.
Rnd 6: Sl st in ch-1 sp, ch 4, dc in
same ch-1 sp, * (V-st, ch 2, V-st) in
corner ch-2 sp, V-st in next V-st and
in ea V-st across to corner ch-2 sp;
rep from * twice, V-st in next V-st
and in ea V-st across to beg ch-4;
join with sl st to 3rd ch of beg ch-4:
36 V-sts.
Rnds 7 and 8: Sl st in ch-1 sp,
ch 4, dc in same ch-1 sp, * V-st in
next V-st and in ea V-st across to
corner ch-2 sp, (V-st, ch 2, V-st) in
corner ch-2 sp; rep from * 3 times,
V-st in next V-st and in ea V-st across
to beg ch-4; join with sl st to 3rd ch
of beg ch-4; fasten off after last rnd:
52 V-sts.

Assembly
Afghan is 7 squares long and 5
squares wide. With ws facing, using
MC, and working through bk lps
only, whipstitch squares tog.

Border
Rnd 1 (rs): With rs facing, join MC
with sl st in any ch-2 sp, ch 1, 4 sc in
same sp, * (sc in next dc and in ea dc
across to joining, sc in sp before
joining, sc in joining, sc in sp after
joining) across to last joining, sc in
next dc and in ea dc across to next
corner ch-2 sp **, 4 sc in corner; rep
from * around, ending last rep at **;
join with sl st to beg sc.
Rnd 2: Ch 3 [counts as first dc],
dc in next sc, * ch 3 [corner made],
dc in next sc and in ea sc across to
first 2 sc of corner 4-sc grp **, dc in
first 2 sc; rep from * around, ending
last rep at **; join with sl st to top of
beg ch-3.
Rnd 3: Ch 3, dc in next dc, * (2 dc,
ch 3, 2 dc) in corner ch-3 sp, dc in
next dc and in ea dc across to next
corner ch-3 sp; rep from * twice,
(2 dc, ch 3, 2 dc) in corner ch-3 sp,
dc in next dc and in ea dc across to
beg ch-3; join with sl st to top of
beg ch-3; fasten off.
Rnd 4: With rs facing, join B in any
corner ch-3 sp with sl st, ch 1,
* 4 sc in corner sp, sc in next dc and
in ea dc across to next corner
ch-3 sp; rep from * around; join with
sl st to beg sc; fasten off.
Rnd 5: With rs facing, join A with
sl st in any corner between 2nd and
3rd sc with sl st, ch 1, * sc in next sc
and in ea sc across to next corner
4-sc grp, sc in first 2 sc **, sc in sp
before next sc; rep from * around,
ending last rep at **; join with sl st
to beg sc; fasten off.

Afghan by Geneva Warren
Dora, Alabama

Purple Starbursts

Start with double crochet stitches in a bold color and then add straightstitches with a doubled strand of a contrasting color for a striking throw.

Materials

Worsted-weight acrylic yarn, approximately:
63 oz. (3,835 yd.) purple, MC
7 oz. (430 yd.) fuchsia, CC
Size H crochet hook or size to obtain gauge
Yarn needle

Finished Size

Approximately 48" x 54"

Gauge

12 dc and 6 rows = 3"

Pattern Stitch

Shell: [(Dc, ch 1) 5 times, dc] in st indicated.

With MC, ch 193.
Row 1 (rs): Dc in 4th ch from hook and in ea ch across: 191 dc.
Row 2: Ch 3 [counts as first dc throughout], turn; dc in next 2 dc, * ch 1, sk next dc, dc in next dc; rep from * across to last 3 dc, dc in last 3 dc: 93 ch-1 sps.
Row 3: Ch 3, turn; dc in next 2 dc, ch 1, sk next ch-1 sp, * (dc in next dc, dc in next ch-1 sp) 3 times, dc in next dc, ch 1, sk next ch-1 sp; rep from * across to last 3 dc, dc in last 3 dc: 24 ch-1 sps.
Row 4: Ch 3, turn; dc in next 2 dc, ch 1, sk next ch-1 sp, * dc in next 3 dc, ch 1, sk next dc, dc in next 3 dc, ch 1, sk next ch-1 sp; rep from * across to last 3 dc, dc in last 3 dc: 47 ch-1 sps.
Row 5: Ch 3, turn; dc in next 2 dc, ch 1, sk next ch-1 sp, * dc in next 3 dc, dc in next ch-1 sp, dc in next 3 dc, ch 1, sk next ch-1 sp; rep from * across to last 3 dc, dc in last 3 dc: 24 ch-1 sps.
Row 6: Ch 3, turn; dc in next 2 dc, * ch 1, sk next ch-1 sp, dc in next dc, (ch 1, sk next dc, dc in next dc) 3 times; rep from * across to last ch-1 sp, ch 1, sk ch-1 sp, dc in last 3 dc.
Rows 7–102: Rep rows 3–6, 24 times.

Row 103: Ch 3, turn; dc in next dc and in ea dc and ch-1 sp across; do not fasten off: 191 dc.

Top Edging

Row 1 (ws): Ch 3 [counts as first dc], turn; dc in next dc and in ea dc across; do not fasten off: 191 dc.
Row 2 (rs): Ch 1, turn; sk first 3 dc, * shell in next dc **, sk next 3 dc, sc in next dc, sk next 3 dc; rep from * across, ending last rep at **, sk next 2 dc, sc in last dc; fasten off: 24 shells.

Bottom Edging

Row 1 (ws): With ws facing, join MC in bottom left corner with sl st, ch 3 [counts as first dc], dc in same dc and in ea dc across; do not fasten off: 191 dc.
Row 2 (rs): Ch 1, turn; sk first 3 dc, * shell in next dc **, sk next 3 dc, sc in next dc, sk next 3 dc; rep from * across, ending last rep at **, sk next 2 dc, sc in last dc; fasten off: 24 shells.

Embroidery

With rs facing and 2 strands of CC, bring needle up in 2nd ch-1 sp on row 4, down in next ch-1 sp; cont straightstitch as est in ea ch-1 sp around center ch-1 sp of Starburst; fasten off: 16 straightstitches.

Referring to photo, work 5 rows of Starbursts in checkerboard pattern on ea end and center of afghan.

Afghan by Margaret E. Gessner Pittsburgh, Pennsylvania

Fan-Stitch Favorite

Knitted in narrow panels, this lovely afghan works up quickly. Be sure to choose four colors that blend well together.

Materials

Worsted-weight acrylic yarn, approximately:
21 oz. (1,140 yd.) burgundy, MC
10½ oz. (570 yd.) dark rose, A
10½ oz. (570 yd.) medium rose, B
10½ oz. (570 yd.) light rose, C
Size 6 knitting needles or size to obtain gauge
Yarn needle

Finished Size

Approximately 45" x 57", without fringe

Gauge

In pat, 15 sts and 30 rows = 4"

Pattern Stitches

Yo [inc]: Wrap yarn around right needle, insert right needle in next st on left needle from left to right, complete k st.
K2tog: Insert right needle into front of next 2 sts from left to right, complete k st.
P2tog: Insert right needle into front of next 2 sts from right to left, complete p st.
P2tog in back: Insert right needle into back of next 2 sts from left to right, complete p st.

One-Fan Panel (Make 2 A and 2 B.)

CO 17 sts.
Row 1 (rs): K across: 17 sts.
Row 2: K 3, p 11, k 3: 17 sts.
Row 3: K 4, yo 10 times, k 3: 27 sts.
Row 4: K 3, k2tog, k 17, k2tog, k 3: 25 sts.
Row 5: K 3, p2tog, p 15, p2tog, k 3: 23 sts.

Row 6: K 3, p2tog, p 13, p2tog in back, k 3: 21 sts.
Row 7: K 3, sl next st as if to k, k 1, psso, k 11, k2tog, k 3: 19 sts.
Row 8: K 3, p2tog, p 9, p2tog in back, k 3: 17 sts.
Rows 9–424: Rep rows 1–8, 52 times; BO after last row.

Two-Fan Panel (Make 2 MC and 1 C.)

CO 34 sts.
Row 1 (rs): K across: 34 sts.
Row 2: K 3, p 11, k 6, p 11, k 3: 34 sts.
Row 3: K 4, yo 10 times, k 7, yo 10 times, k 3: 54 sts.
Row 4: K 3, k2tog, k 17, k2tog, k 6, k2tog, k 17, k2tog, k 3: 50 sts.
Row 5: K 3, p2tog, p 15, p2tog, k 6, p2tog, p 15, p2tog, k 3: 46 sts.
Row 6: K 3, p2tog, p 13, p2tog in back, k 6, p2tog, p 13, p2tog in back, k 3: 42 sts.

Row 7: K 3, sl next st as if to k, k 1, psso, k 11, k2tog, k 6, sl next st as if to k, k 1, psso, k 11, k2tog, k 3: 38 sts.
Row 8: K 3, p2tog, p 9, p2tog in back, k 6, p2tog, p 9, p2tog in back, k 3: 34 sts.
Rows 9–424: Rep rows 1–8, 52 times; BO after last row.

Assembly

With rs tog, weave strips tog in foll color sequence: MC, A, B, C, B, A, MC.

Fringe

For ea tassel, referring to page 159 of General Directions, cut 2 (10") lengths MC. Working across short ends, knot 1 tassel in ea st.

Afghan by Patricia Heasley
Hadley, Pennsylvania

Artful Aztec

Three panels of afghan stitch make this geometric design. Since the side panels are mirror images, just flip the chart for the second side.

Materials

Worsted-weight acrylic yarn, approximately:
49 oz. (2,730 yd.) black, MC
7 oz. (390 yd.) teal, A
28 oz. (1,560 yd.) white, B
10½ oz. (585 yd.) purple, C
Size I afghan hook or size to obtain gauge
Size I crochet hook or size to obtain gauge
Yarn needle

Finished Size

Approximately 50" x 73"

Gauge

21 sts and 16 rows = 4"

Note: See page 148 for afghan st directions. To change colors in afghan st: **Step 1:** Drop yarn to ws of work, insert hook under next vertical bar and pull up lp with new color. Do not carry yarn over more than 3 sts. **Step 2:** Yo and pull through 2 lps on hook until 1 lp of current color rem on hook, drop yarn to ws of work, pick up new color, yo and pull through 2 lps on hook.

Left Panel

With afghan hook and MC, ch 88.
Rows 1–3: Work 3 rows of afghan st: 88 sts.
Note: Read **Side Panel Chart** from right to left.
Rows 4–60: Foll **Side Panel Chart** on page 48: 88 sts.
Rows 61–284: Rep rows 5–60, 4 times.
Rows 285–287: Work 3 rows of afghan st: 88 sts.
Row 288: Sl st in ea vertical bar across; fasten off.

Right Panel

With afghan hook and MC, ch 88.
Rows 1–3: Work 3 rows of afghan st: 88 sts.
Note: Read **Side Panel Chart** from left to right.
Rows 4–60: Foll **Side Panel Chart** on page 48: 88 sts.
Rows 61–284: Rep rows 5–60, 4 times.

Rows 285–287: Work 3 rows of afghan st: 88 sts.
Row 288: Sl st in ea vertical bar across; fasten off.

Center Panel

With afghan hook and MC, ch 84.
Rows 1–3: Work 3 rows of afghan st: 84 sts.
Note: Read **Center Panel Chart** from right to left.
Rows 4–60: Foll **Center Panel Chart** on page 49: 84 sts.
Rows 61–284: Rep rows 5–60, 4 times.
Rows 285–287: Work 3 rows of afghan st: 88 sts.
Row 288: Sl st in ea vertical bar across; fasten off.

Assembly

With rs tog and using MC, whip-stitch panels tog.

Border

Rnd 1 (ws): With ws facing and using crochet hook, join MC in back of 3rd st of row 3 with sl st, ch 1, sc in same st and in ea st across to corner, * 3 sc in corner, sc in ea st across to next corner; rep from * around; join with sl st to beg sc.
Rnds 2 and 3: Ch 1, sc in back of next st of next row, sc in ea st across to corner, * 3 sc in corner; sc in ea st across to next corner; rep from * around; join with sl st to beg sc.
Rnd 4: Ch 1, sc in next sc and in ea sc across to corner, * 3 sc in corner; sc in ea st across to next corner; rep from * around; join with sl st to beg sc.

Afghan by Barbara Pawelko
Mt. Prospect, Illinois

Repeat

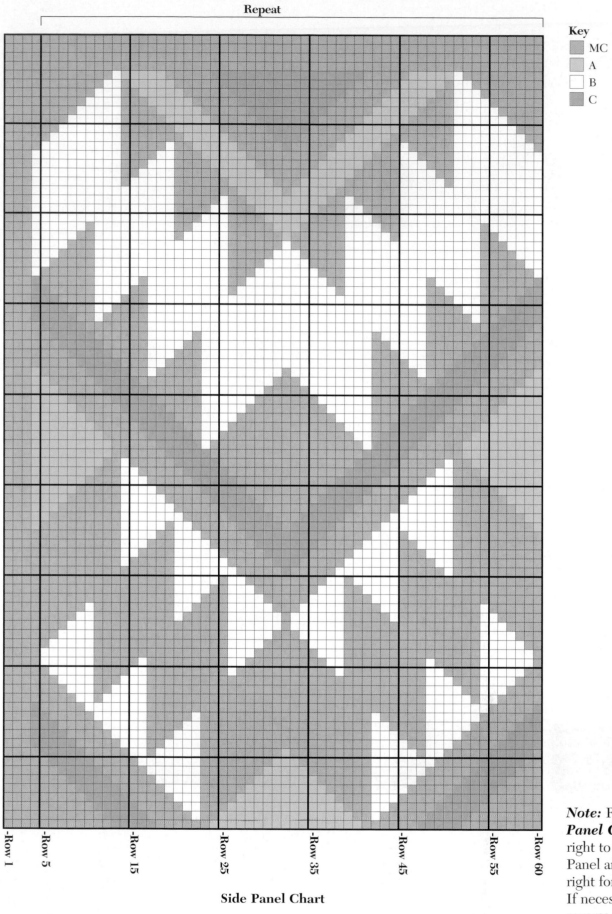

Key
- MC
- A
- B
- C

-Row 1　-Row 5　-Row 15　-Row 25　-Row 35　-Row 45　-Row 55　-Row 60

Side Panel Chart

Note: Read ***Side Panel Chart*** from right to left for Left Panel and from left to right for Right Panel. If necessary, make reverse photocopy of ***Side Panel Chart.***

48

Repeat

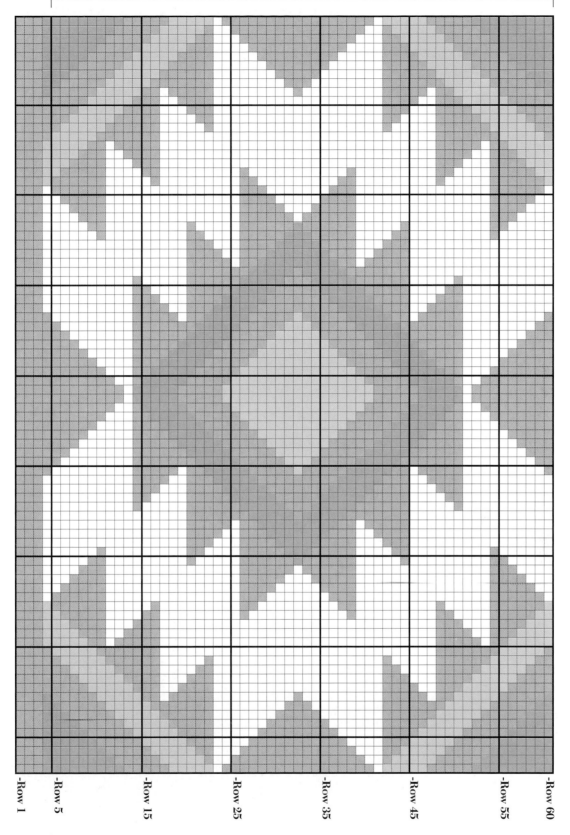

-Row 1 -Row 5 -Row 15 -Row 25 -Row 35 -Row 45 -Row 55 -Row 60

Center Panel Chart

49

Irish Trellis

Use traditional textured Aran stitches to make lovely lattice panels.
Slip-stitch pink stripes to accent the blue-and-white color scheme.

Materials

Worsted-weight acrylic yarn,
approximately:
69 oz. (3,450 yd.) blue, MC
6 oz. (300 yd.) cream, A
3 oz. (150 yd.) pink, B
Size J crochet hook or size to
obtain gauge

Finished Size

Approximately 55" x 66"

Gauge

In pat, 1½ Vs and 4 rows = 4"

Pattern Stitch

Cable: Ch 3, sk 2 sts, sc in next st,
turn; sc in ea ch back to sc, sl st in
sc, turn; sc in 2 sk sts, sc in same st
as first sc of cable.

Note: Afghan is worked sideways. To
change colors, work last yo of prev st
with new color, dropping prev color
to ws of work. Do not carry yarn
across row.

With MC, ch 192.
Row 1(rs): Sc in 2nd ch from hook
and in ea ch across: 191 sc.
Row 2: Ch 1, turn; working in ft lps
only, sc in ea sc across.
Row 3: Ch 1, turn; sc in first sc,
sc in next sc, cable across: 63 cables.
Row 4 (ws): Ch 1, turn; working in
front of cables, sc in ea st across,
change to A in last st: 191 sc.
Row 5: Ch 4 [counts as tr through-
out], turn; * sk next sc, tr in next sc,
working behind tr just made, tr in
sk sc; rep from * across to last sc,
tr in last sc, change to MC in last st:
94 crossed trs.

Row 6: Ch 1, turn; sc in ea st across:
191 sc.
Rows 7 and 8: Rep rows 3 and 4
once; do not change colors at end of
row 4.
Row 9: Ch 1, turn; working in bk lps
only, sc in ea sc across: 191 sc.
Row 10: Ch 4, turn; * sk next 3 sts,
tr in next st, working in front of tr
just made, tr in 3 sk sts **, sk next st,
tr in next 3 sts, working behind
3 tr just made, tr in sk st; rep from *
across, ending last rep at **, tr in last
st: 23½ Vs.
Row 11: Ch 4, turn; * sk next 3 sts,
tr in next st, working behind tr just
made, tr in 3 sk sts **, sk next st,
tr in next 3 sts, working in front of
3 tr just made, tr in sk st; rep from *
across, ending last rep at **, tr in last
st: 23½ Vs.
Rows 12–14: Rep rows 10 and 11
once, then rep row 10 once more.
Row 15: Ch 1, turn; sc in ea st
across: 191 sc.
Rows 16–107: Rep rows 2–15,
6 times, then rep rows 2–9 once;
fasten off.

With rs facing, join B in unused lp
of first st on row 2 with sl st, sl st in
ea st across; fasten off. Rep for row 9
and ea rep of rows 2 and 9.

Border

Rnd 1 (rs): With rs facing, join MC
in top right corner with sl st, ch 1,
2 sc in same corner, sc in ea st across
to next corner, * 3 sc in corner,
sc evenly across to next corner; rep
from * around; join with sl st to
beg sc.
Rnds 2–5: Ch 1, sc in same sc and
in ea sc across to corner, * 3 sc in
corner, sc in ea sc across to next
corner; rep from * around; join with
sl st to beg sc.
Rnd 6: Working in bk lps only, sl st
in next sc and in ea sc around; join
with sl st to beg sl st; fasten off.

Afghan by Mary Genin
Laguna Hills, California

Scalloped Ripple

This unusual ripple pattern has no increases or decreases.
Instead, it combines triple crochet and chain stitches
to create a shaped piece.

Materials

Worsted-weight acrylic yarn,
approximately:
24 oz. (1,360 yd.) green-and-
purple multicolored, MC
10½ oz. (570 yd.) lavender, A
10½ oz. (570 yd.) light coral, B
10½ oz. (570 yd.) coral, C
10½ oz. (570 yd.) dark green, D
10½ oz. (570 yd.) sage green, E
10½ oz. (570 yd.) gray, F
10½ oz. (570 yd.) navy, G
Size G crochet hook or size to
obtain gauge
Yarn needle

Finished Size

Approximately 69" x 74"

Gauge

21 tr and 7 rows = 6"

Note: All rows are worked with rs
facing.

With MC, ch 374.
Row 1 (rs): Tr in 4th ch from hook
and in next 6 chs, * ch 4 [counts as tr
throughout], sl st in next ch, sk 3 chs,
tr in next 4 chs, ch 4, sl st in next ch,
sk 3 chs, tr in next 2 chs, (ch 4, sl st in
next ch, sk 3 chs, tr in next ch) twice,
ch 4, sl st in next 3 chs [mark middle
sl st], (ch 4, tr in next ch, sk 3 chs,
sl st in next ch) twice, ch 4, tr in next
2 chs, sk 3 chs, sl st in next ch, ch 4,
tr in next 4 chs, sk 3 chs, sl st in next
ch, ch 4 **, tr in next 10 chs; rep
from * 4 times, then rep from * to **
once, tr in last 8 chs; fasten off.
Row 2 (rs): With rs facing, join A in
top right corner with sl st, ch 4, tr in

next 7 tr, * ch 4, sl st in top of next
ch-4, tr in next 4 tr, ch 4, sl st in top
of next ch-4, tr in next 2 tr, (ch 4,
sl st in top of next ch-4, tr in next tr)
twice, ch 4, sl st in top of next ch-4,
tr in marked sl st, (sl st in top of next
ch-4, ch 4, tr in next tr) twice, sl st in
top of next ch-4, ch 4, tr in next 2 tr,
sl st in top of next ch-4, ch 4, tr in
next 4 tr, sl st in top of next ch-4,
ch 4 **, tr in next 10 tr; rep from *
4 times, then rep from * to ** once,
tr in last 8 tr; fasten off.
Row 3: Join MC in top right corner
with sl st, ch 4, tr in next 7 tr, * ch 4,
sl st in top of next ch-4, tr in next
4 tr, ch 4, sl st in top of next ch-4,
tr in next 2 tr, (ch 4, sl st in top of
next ch-4, tr in next tr) 3 times,
(sl st in top of next ch-4, ch 4, tr in
next tr) twice, sl st in top of next
ch-4, ch 4, tr in next 2 tr, sl st in top
of next ch-4, ch 4, tr in next 4 tr, sl st
in top of next ch-4, ch 4 **, tr in next
10 tr; rep from * 4 times, then rep
from * to ** once, tr in last 8 tr;
fasten off.
Rows 4–82: Rep row 3, 79 times,
working in foll color sequence:
* 1 row ea B, C, MC, C **, B, MC,
D, E, F, G, A, F, E, D, MC; rep
from * 4 times, then rep from * to **
once.
Row 83: Sk first 8 tr, * join B in top
of next ch-4 with sl st, tr in next 4 tr,
ch 4, sl st in top of next ch-4, tr in
next 2 tr, (ch 4, sl st in top of next
ch-4, tr in next tr) 3 times, (sl st in
top of next ch-4, ch 4, tr in next tr)
twice, sl st in top of next ch-4, ch 4,
tr in next 2 tr, sl st in top of next
ch-4, ch 4, tr in next 4 tr, sl st in top
of next ch-4; fasten off; sk next 10 tr;
rep from * across.

Row 84: Sk first 13 sts, * join MC in
top of next ch-4 with sl st, tr in next
2 tr, (ch 4, sl st in top of next ch-4,
tr in next tr) 3 times, (sl st in top of
next ch-4, ch 4, tr in next tr) twice,
sl st in top of next ch-4, ch 4, tr in
next 2 tr, sl st in top of next ch-4;
fasten off; sk next 20 sts; rep from *
across.
Row 85: Sk first 16 sts, * join D in
top of next ch-4 with sl st, tr in next
tr, (ch 4, sl st in top of next ch-4,
tr in next tr) twice, (sl st in top of
next ch-4, ch 4, tr in next tr) twice,
sl st in top of next ch-4; fasten off;
sk next 26 sts; rep from * across.
Row 86: Working 2 rows below,
sk first 20 sts, * join E in top of next
ch-4 with sl st, tr in next tr, sl st in
top of next ch-4; fasten off; sk next
34 sts; rep from * across.
Row 87: Sk first 18 sts, * join E in
top of next ch-4 with sl st, tr in next
tr and in next 4 sts, sl st in top of
next ch-4; fasten off; sk next 30 sts;
rep from * across.
Row 88: With rs facing, join D in
bottom left corner with sl st, ch 4,
tr in next 7 tr, * sl st in top of next
ch-4, ch 4, tr in next 4 tr, sl st in top
of next ch-4, ch 4, tr in next 2 tr,
sl st in top of next ch-4, ch 4, tr in
next tr, sl st in top of next ch-4; fasten off; sk next 5 sts, join D in top of
next ch-4 with sl st, tr in next tr,
ch 4, sl st in top of next ch-4, tr in
next 2 tr, ch 4, sl st in top of next
ch-4, tr in next 4 tr, ch 4, sl st in top
of next ch-4 **, tr in next 10 sts; rep
from * across, ending last rep at **,
tr in last 8 sts; fasten off.

(continued)

Row 89: With rs facing, join D in bottom left corner with sl st, ch 4, tr in next 7 tr, * sl st in top of next ch-4, ch 4, tr in next 4 tr, sl st in top of next ch-4, ch 4, tr in next 2 tr, sl st in top of next ch-4; fasten off; sk next 9 sts, join D in top of next ch-4 with sl st, tr in next 2 tr, ch 4, sl st in top of next ch-4, tr in next 4 tr, ch 4, sl st in top of next ch-4 **, tr in next 10 sts; rep from * across, ending last rep at **, tr in last 8 sts; fasten off.

Row 90: With rs facing, join F in bottom left corner with sl st, ch 4, tr in next 7 tr, * sl st in top of next ch-4, ch 4, tr in next 4 tr, sl st in top of next ch-4; fasten off; sk next 15 sts, join D in top of next ch-4 with sl st, tr in next 4 tr, ch 4, sl st in top of next ch-4 **, tr in next 10 sts; rep from * across, ending last rep at **, tr in last 8 sts; fasten off.

Row 91: With rs facing, join A in bottom left corner with sl st, ch 4, tr in next 7 tr, sl st in top of next ch-4; fasten off; * sk next 25 sts, join D in top of next ch-4 with sl st **, tr in next 10 tr, sl st in top of next ch-4; fasten off; rep from * across, ending last rep at **, tr in last 8 sts; do not fasten off.

Border

Rnd 1 (rs): Ch 4, 4 tr in same st, tr evenly across to next corner, * 5 tr in corner, sc evenly across to next corner; rep from * around; join with sl st to top of beg ch-4; fasten off.

Rnd 2: With rs facing, join G in top right corner with sl st, ch 3 [counts as dc], dc in same st, 2 dc in next tr, * dc in next tr and in ea tr across to last 2 tr, 2 dc in next tr **, 2 dc in corner tr, 2 dc in next tr; rep from

* around, ending last rep at **; join with sl st to beg ch-3; fasten off.

Rnd 3: With rs facing, join MC in top right corner with sl st, ch 3, dc in same dc and in next dc, 2 dc in next dc, dc in ea dc across to last 3 dc, * (2 dc in next dc, dc in next dc) 3 times, dc in ea dc across to last 3 dc; rep from * around, 2 dc in next dc, dc in next dc; join with sl st to beg ch-3; do not fasten off.

Rnd 4: Ch 3, dc in same dc and in next dc, 2 dc in next dc, dc in ea dc across to last 3 dc, * (2 dc in next dc, dc in next dc) 3 times, dc in ea dc across to last 3 dc; rep from * around, 2 dc in next dc, dc in next dc; join with sl st to beg ch-3; fasten off.

Afghan by Kathy Blakely
Ririe, Idaho

Paisley Perfection

Renew the classic paisley motif with today's soft colors. Edge each afghan-stitched panel with a honeycomb of post stitches.

Materials

Worsted-weight acrylic yarn,
approximately:
24 oz. (1,360 yd.) cream, MC
24½ oz. (1,390 yd.) seafoam, A
12 oz. (680 yd.) teal, B
3 oz. (170 yd.) rose, C
3 oz. (170 yd.) light rose, D
Size J afghan hook or size to
    obtain gauge
Size K crochet hook or size to
    obtain gauge

Finished Size

Approximately 43" x 58", without
fringe

Gauge

In afghan st, 12 sts and 10 rows = 3"
In dc, 10 sts and 10 rows = 3"

Pattern Stitch

FPdc: Yo, insert hook from front to
back around st indicated, yo and pull
up lp, (yo and pull through 2 lps) twice.

Note: See page 148 for afghan st
directions. To change colors in
afghan st: **Step 1:** Drop yarn to ws of
work, insert hook under next vertical
bar and pull up lp with new color.
Do not carry yarn over more than
3 sts. **Step 2:** Yo and pull through
2 lps on hook until 1 lp of current
color rem on hook, drop yarn to ws
of work, pick up new color, yo and
pull through 2 lps on hook.

Side Paisley Panel
(Make 2.)

With afghan hook and MC, ch 28.
Rows 1–4: Work 4 rows of afghan
st: 28 sts.
Rows 5–99: Foll *Chart:* 28 sts.
Rows 100–190: Rep rows 25–99
once, then rep rows 25–40 once:
28 sts.
Rows 191–194: Work 4 rows of
afghan st: 28 sts.
Row 195: Sl st in ea vertical bar
across; fasten off.

Edging
Row 1 (rs): With rs facing and crochet hook, join MC in top left corner with sl st, ch 1, sc in same st and
in ea st across to next corner; fasten
off: 194 sc.
Row 2: With rs facing, join MC in
top left corner with sl st, ch 1, working in bk lps only, sc in same sc and
in next sc, (dc in next vertical bar,
sc in next 2 sc) across to next corner;
fasten off: 64 dc.
Row 3: With rs facing, join A in top
left corner with sl st, ch 1, working
in bk lps only, sc in same sc, (FPdc
around next st, sc in next 2 sts)
across to last 4 sts, FPdc around next
st, sc in last 3 sts; fasten off: 64 FPdc.

Row 4: With rs facing, join A in top
left corner with sl st, ch 1, working
in bk lps only, sc in same sc and in
next 2 sts, (FPdc around next st,
sc in next 2 sts) across to last 2 sts,
FPdc around next st, sc in last st;
fasten off: 64 FPdc.
Row 5: With rs facing, join A in top
left corner with sl st, ch 1, working
in bk lps only, sc in same sc and in
next st, (FPdc around next st, sc in
next 2 sts) across; fasten off:
64 FPdc.
Rows 6–13: Rep rows 3–5 twice,
then rep rows 3 and 4 once, foll
color sequence: 3 rows B, 5 rows A.
Row 14 (rs): With rs facing, join
MC in bottom right corner with

sl st, ch 1, sc in same st and in ea st across to next corner; fasten off: 194 sc.

Rows 15–26: Rep rows 2–13 once, joining yarn in bottom right corner.

Center Paisley Panel
(Make 1.)
With afghan hook and MC, ch 28.

Rows 1 and 2: Work 2 rows of afghan st: 28 sts.

Rows 3–43: Foll *Chart,* work rows 59–99: 28 sts.

Rows 44–193: Rep rows 25–99 twice: 28 sts.

Row 194: Work 1 row of afghan st: 28 sts.

Row 195: Sl st in ea vertical bar across; fasten off.

Edging
Work same as edging for Side Paisley Panel.

Assembly
With rs facing and using A and working in ft lps only, sl st panels tog.

Border
With rs facing and crochet hook, join A in top right corner with sl st, ch 1, 3 sc in same st, * (sc evenly across to next MC section, change to MC, sc across MC section, change to A) 3 times, sc evenly across to corner, 3 sc in corner, sc evenly across to next corner; rep from * around; join with sl st to beg sc; fasten off.

Fringe
For ea tassel, referring to page 159 of General Directions, cut 5 (14") lengths of yarn. Working across short ends and matching colors, knot 1 tassel in approximately every 3rd sc.

Afghan by Dorothy Warrell
Granville, Ohio

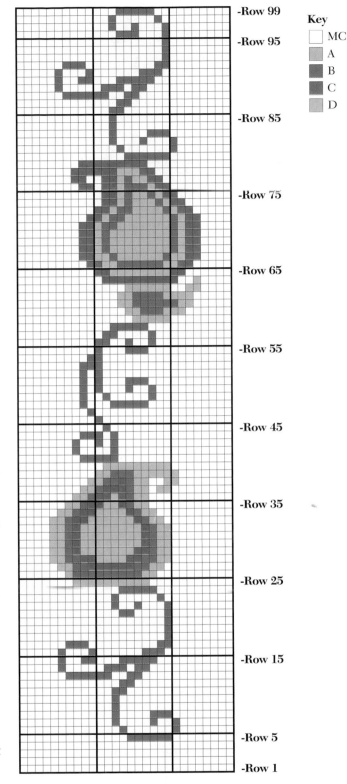

-Row 99
-Row 95
-Row 85
-Row 75
-Row 65
-Row 55
-Row 45
-Row 35
-Row 25
-Row 15
-Row 5
-Row 1

Key
MC
A
B
C
D

Paisley Panel Chart

Afghan-Stitch Aran

Puffy little picot stitches add dimension to an elegant throw. This afghan is easier to make than a traditional Aran pattern because it combines just two stitches.

Materials

Worsted-weight acrylic yarn, approximately:
66½ oz. (3,705 yd.) cream
Size I afghan hook or size to obtain gauge
Size I crochet hook or size to obtain gauge
Yarn needle

Finished Size

Approximately 46" x 62", without fringe

Gauge

18 sts and 11½ rows = 4"

Note: See page 148 for afghan st directions.

Right Diagonal Panel (Make 1.)

With afghan hook, ch 25.
Rows 1 and 2: Work 2 rows of afghan st: 25 sts.
Row 3: Step 1: Referring to *Right Diagonal Chart* on page 60, pull up 2 lps, ch 4 [picot made], (pull up 4 lps, ch 4) 5 times, pull up 2 lps: 25 lps on hook. **Step 2:** Yo and pull through first lp on hook, * yo and pull through 2 lps on hook; rep from * across.
Rows 4–6: Cont foll *Right Diagonal Chart* as est.
Rows 7–179: Rep rows 3–6, 43

times, then rep row 3 once.
Row 180: Work 1 row of afghan st.
Row 181: Sl st in ea vertical bar across; fasten off.

Left Diagonal Panel (Make 1.)

With afghan hook, ch 25.
Rows 1 and 2: Work 2 rows of afghan st: 25 sts.
Row 3: Step 1: Referring to *Left Diagonal Chart* on page 60, pull up 2 lps, ch 4 [picot made], (pull up 4 lps, ch 4) 5 times, pull up 2 lps: 25 lps on hook. **Step 2:** Yo and pull through first lp on hook, * yo and pull through 2 lps on hook; rep from * across.
Rows 4–6: Cont foll *Left Diagonal Chart* as est.
Rows 7–179: Rep rows 3–6, 43 times, then rep row 3 once.
Row 180: Work 1 row of afghan st.
Row 181: Sl st in ea vertical bar across; fasten off.

Diamond Panel (Make 2.)

With afghan hook, ch 53.
Rows 1 and 2: Work 2 rows of afghan st: 53 sts.
Row 3: Step 1: Referring to *Diamond Chart* on page 60, pull up 6 lps, ch 4 [picot made], (pull up 8 lps, ch 4) 5 times, pull up 6 lps: 53 lps on hook. **Step 2:** Yo and pull through first lp on hook, * yo and pull through 2 lps on hook; rep from * across.
Rows 4–11: Cont foll *Diamond Chart* as est.
Rows 12–179: Rep rows 4–11, 21 times.

(continued)

Row 180: Work 1 row of afghan st.
Row 181: Sl st in ea vertical bar across; fasten off.

Cable Panel (Make 1.)
With afghan hook, ch 52.
Rows 1 and 2: Work 2 rows of afghan st: 52 sts.
Row 3: Step 1: Referring to *Cable Chart,* (pull up 5 lps, ch 4 [picot made]) twice, (pull up 7 lps, ch 4, pull up 5 lps, ch 4) 3 times, pull up 5 lps: 52 lps on hook. **Step 2:** Yo and pull through first lp on hook, * yo and pull through 2 lps on hook; rep from * across.
Rows 4–15: Cont foll *Cable Chart* as est.

Rows 16–179: Rep rows 5–14, 16 times, then rep rows 5–8 once.
Row 180: Work 1 row of afghan st.
Row 181: Sl st in ea vertical bar across; fasten off.

Assembly
With ws facing, whipstitch panels tog in foll sequence: Diamond Panel, Left Diagonal Panel, Cable Panel, Right Diagonal Panel, Diamond Panel.

Border
With rs facing and using crochet hook, join yarn in top right corner with sl st, ch 1, * (sc, ch 2, sc) in corner, (ch 2, sk next st, sc in next st) across to next corner; rep from * around; join with sl st to beg sc; fasten off.

Fringe
For ea tassel, referring to page 159 of General Directions, cut 4 (10") lengths of yarn. Working across short ends, knot 1 tassel in ea ch-2 sp.

Afghan by Elizabeth Klaczak
Bethel Park, Pennsylvania

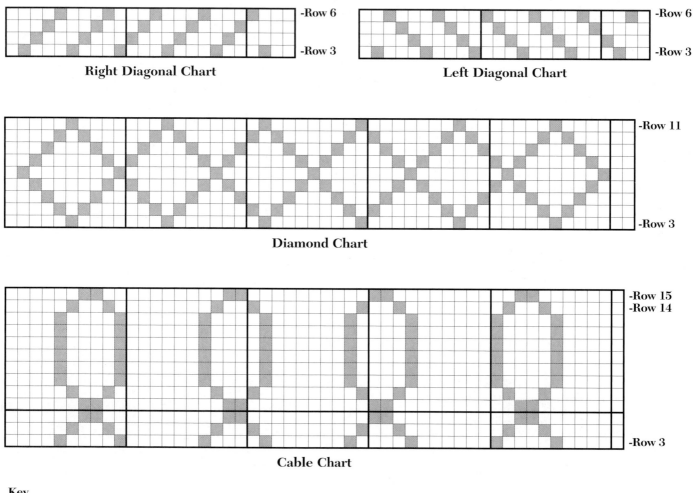

Right Diagonal Chart

Left Diagonal Chart

Diamond Chart

Cable Chart

Key

■ picot
□ afghan st

Diamonds and Rings

Create some crochet magic with these linking rings. Finish the trick with lattice panels and a flourish of fringe.

Materials ⬤⬤

Worsted-weight acrylic yarn, approximately:
24 oz. (1,360 yd.) burgundy, MC
24 oz. (1,360 yd.) white, A
24 oz. (1,360 yd.) rose, B
Size I crochet hook or size to obtain gauge
Yarn needle

Finished Size

Approximately 44" x 65", without fringe

Gauge

In Diamond pat, 12 sts and 9 rows = 3½"

Pattern Stitches

Picot: Insert hook in st indicated and pull up lp, (yo and pull through 1 lp) 3 times, yo and pull through both lps on hook.

FPtr: Yo twice, insert hook from front to back around st indicated, yo and pull up lp, (yo and pull through 2 lps) 3 times; sk st behind FPtr.

FPtr-cl: * Yo twice, insert hook from front to back around st indicated, yo and pull up lp, (yo and pull through 2 lps) twice; rep from * once, yo and pull through all 3 lps on hook; sk st behind FPtr-cl.

Note: To change colors, work last yo of prev st with new color, dropping prev color to ws of work. Do not carry yarn across row.

Ring Panel (Make 6.)

First Ring
With MC, ch 14, join with sl st to form ring.
Rnd 1 (rs): Ch 3 [counts as first dc throughout], 23 dc in ring; join with sl st to top of beg ch-3; fasten off: 24 dc.

Next Ring
With A, ch 14; with rs of prev Ring facing, thread beg chain through center of prev ring; join with sl st to form ring.
Rnd 1: Ch 3, 23 dc in ring; join with sl st to top of beg ch-3; fasten off: 24 dc.

Cont joining Rings as est, alternating colors, until 49 Rings are joined.

Half Ring (Make 2.)
With A, ch 10.
Row 1 (rs): 2 dc in 4th ch from hook and in next 5 chs, dc in last ch; fasten off: 14 dc.

Edging
Rnd 1 (rs): With rs facing and working in bk lps only, join MC in any dc of First Ring with sl st, ch 3 [counts as dc], * holding Half Ring under First Ring and working in next st of First Ring and around last dc of Half Ring, hdc in next st, (3 dc, hdc) in same st as joining [corner made], hdc in next st, sc in next 3 sts, hdc in next st, holding Half Ring on top of First Ring and working around first dc of Half Ring and in next st of First Ring, hdc in next st, (3 dc, hdc) in same st as joining [corner made], (hdc in next st, sc in next 2 sts, hdc in next st, dc in next st, sc in next 3 sts of Next Ring, dc in next st of Next Ring) across to last Ring, hdc in next st, sc in next 2 sts, hdc in next st; rep from * once; join with sl st to top of beg ch-3; fasten off.

Note: Beg working in rows.
Row 1 (rs): With rs facing, join MC in bottom right corner with sl st, ch 3, working bk lps only, work 224 dc evenly across to next corner; fasten off: 225 dc.
Row 2 (rs): With rs facing, join MC in top left corner with sl st, ch 3, working in bk lps only, work 224 dc evenly across to next corner; fasten off: 225 dc.

Diamond Panel (Make 5.)

Row 1 (rs): With rs facing, join B in bottom right corner of Ring Panel with sl st, ch 1, sc in same st and in next 3 dc, (picot in next dc, sc in next 3 dc) across to last 5 dc, picot in next dc, sc in last 4 dc: 55 picots.
Row 2: Ch 3 [counts as first dc throughout], turn; dc in next st and in ea st across: 225 dc.
Row 3: Ch 1, turn; sc in first 2 dc, picot in next dc, sc in next dc, FPtr-cl beg around 3rd sc 2 rows below and ending around 2nd sc after first picot 2 rows below, * sc in next dc, picot in next dc, sc in next dc **, FPtr-cl beg around same sc 2 rows below as end of last FPtr-cl and ending around 2nd sc after next picot 2 rows below; rep from * across, ending last rep at **, sc in last dc: 56 picots and 55 FPtr-cls.
Row 4: Rep row 2.
Row 5: Ch 1, turn; sc in first 2 dc, FPtr around FPtr-cl 2 rows below, * sc in next dc, picot in next dc, sc in next dc **, FPtr-cl beg around last FPtr-cl 2 rows below and ending around next FPtr-cl 2 rows below; rep from * across, ending last rep at **, FPtr around last FPtr-cl 2 rows below, sc in last 2 dc: 55 picots and 54 FPtr-cls.
Row 6: Rep row 2.
Row 7: Ch 1, turn; sc in first 2 dc, picot in next dc, sc in next dc, FPtr-cl beg around FPtr 2 rows below and ending around next FPtr-cl 2 rows below, * sc in next dc, picot in next dc, sc in next dc **, FPtr-cl beg around last FPtr-cl 2 rows below and ending around next FPtr-cl 2 rows below; rep from * across, ending last rep at ** and ending last FPtr-cl around last FPtr, sc in last dc: 56 picots and 55 FPtr-cls.
Rows 8 and 9: Rep rows 4 and 5 once; fasten off after last row.

Assembly

With rs tog and using MC, whip-stitch 5 Ring/Diamond Panels tog, then join Ring Panel.

Edging

Row 1 (rs): With rs facing, join A in top right corner with sl st, ch 1, sc in same corner, work 150 sc evenly across to next corner: 151 sc.

Row 2: Ch 1, turn; sc in first sc, * ch 3, sk 2 sc, sc in next sc; rep from * across.

Row 3: Turn; sl st in first 2 chs, (ch 3, sc in next ch-3 sp) across; fasten off.

Row 4 (rs): With rs facing, join A in bottom left corner with sl st, ch 1, sc in same corner, work 150 sc evenly across to next corner: 151 sc.

Rows 5 and 6: Rep rows 2 and 3.

Fringe

For ea tassel, referring to page 159 of General Directions, cut 6 (10") lengths of yarn. Working across short ends, knot 1 tassel in ea ch-3 sp.

Afghan by Carla Kisielnicki
McKeesport, Pennsylvania

Rippling Shells

Simple shell stitches become something special when combined with a ripple pattern. Skipped stitches on each side form scalloped edges.

Materials

Worsted-weight acrylic yarn, approximately:
30 oz. (1,500 yd.) peach
Size H crochet hook or size to obtain gauge

Finished Size

Approximately 38" x 48", without fringe

Gauge

In pat, 3 shells and 6½ rows = 3½"

Pattern Stitches

Shell: (2 dc, ch 1, 2 dc) in st indicated.
Cl: Dc in next 4 sts, drop lp from hook, insert hook in first dc of 4-dc grp and pull dropped lp through.

Ch 202.
Row 1 (rs): Dc in 4th ch from hook and in next 2 chs, sk next 2 chs, shell in next ch, (sk next 3 chs, shell in next ch) 3 times, * sk next 2 chs, dc in next 2 chs, (dc, ch 1, dc) in next ch, dc in next 2 chs, sk next 2 chs **, (shell in next ch, sk next 3 chs) 4 times, dc in next ch, (sk next 2 chs, dc in next ch) 3 times, (sk next 3 chs, shell in next ch) 4 times; rep from * across, ending last rep at **, (shell in next ch, sk next 3 chs) 3 times, shell in next ch, sk next 2 chs, dc in last 4 chs: 32 shells.
Row 2: Ch 3 [counts as first dc throughout], turn; dc in next 3 dc, * shell in top [ch-1 sp] of next 4 shells, sk next 2 dc, dc in next 3 dc, shell in next ch-1 sp, dc in next 3 dc,

shell in top of next 4 shells, sk next 2 dc **, cl in next 4 dc; rep from * across, ending last rep at **, dc in last 4 dc: 36 shells.
Row 3: Ch 1, turn; sl st in first 5 dc, ch 3 [counts as dc], dc in next dc, sk next ch-1 sp, dc in next 2 dc, * shell in top of next 3 shells, sk next 3 dc, shell in next dc, sk next 2 dc, dc in next dc, shell in top of shell, dc in next dc, sk 2 dc, shell in next dc and in top of next 3 shells **, dc in top of next shell, sk next dc, dc in next dc, sk cl, dc in next dc, dc in top of next shell; rep from * across, ending last rep at **, sk 2 dc, dc in next 2 dc, sk next ch-1 sp, dc in next 2 dc; leave rem 4 dc unworked: 36 shells.

Rep rows 2 and 3 alternately until piece measures approximately 48", ending with row 2; do not fasten off.

Border

Row 1 (ws): With ws facing and working in ends of rows, sc evenly across to next corner; fasten off.
Row 2 (rs): With rs facing, join yarn in top left corner with sl st, ch 1, working in ends of rows, sc evenly across to next corner; fasten off.

Fringe

For ea tassel, referring to page 159 of General Directions, cut 2 (12") lengths of yarn. Knot tassels evenly across short ends.

Afghan by Blanche L. Hoover
Danville, Indiana

Bargello Beauty

This lush afghan steals its look from needlepoint. Work the beautifully colored flame shapes in three panels of afghan stitch.

Materials

Worsted-weight acrylic yarn, approximately:
21 oz. (1,280 yd.) cream, MC
17½ oz. (975 yd.) dark blue, A
17½ oz. (975 yd.) medium blue, B
10½ oz. (585 yd.) light blue, C
7 oz. (390 yd.) dark purple, D
7 oz. (390 yd.) purple, E
7 oz. (390 yd.) lavender, F
7 oz. (390 yd.) burgundy, G
7 oz. (390 yd.) medium rose, H
3½ oz. (195 yd.) light rose, I
3½ oz. (195 yd.) gold, J
Size H afghan hook or size to obtain gauge
Size H crochet hook or size to obtain gauge
Yarn needle

Finished Size

Approximately 52" x 75"

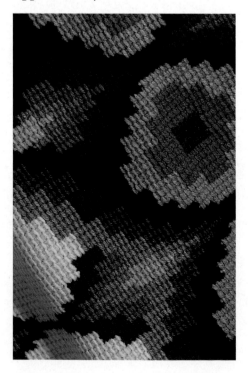

Gauge

33 sts and 23 rows = 6"

Note: See page 148 for afghan st directions. To change colors in afghan st: **Step 1:** Drop yarn to ws of work, insert hook under next vertical bar and pull up lp with new color. Do not carry yarn over more than 3 sts. **Step 2:** Yo and pull through 2 lps on hook until 1 lp of current color rem on hook, drop yarn to ws of work, pick up new color, yo and pull through 2 lps on hook.

Center Panel

With afghan hook and B, ch 91.
Rows 1–3: Work 3 rows of afghan st, change to MC in last st of last row: 91 sts.
Row 4: Work 1 row of afghan st: 91 sts.
Rows 5–73: Foll **Center Panel Chart** on page 69: 91 sts.
Rows 74–257: Rep rows 28–73, 4 times.
Note: Turn **Center Panel Chart** upside down for rows 258–285.
Rows 258–285: Reading **Center Panel Chart** upside down, rep rows 28–1 once.
Row 286: Sl st in ea vertical bar across; fasten off.

Left Panel

With afghan hook and B, ch 96.
Rows 1–3: Work 3 rows of afghan st, change to MC in last st of last row: 96 sts.
Note: Read **Side Panel Chart** from right to left.
Rows 4–73: Foll **Side Panel Chart** on page 68: 96 sts.
Rows 74–257: Rep rows 28–73, 4 times.
Rows 258–285: Foll **Side Panel Chart.**

Row 286: Sl st in ea vertical bar across; fasten off.

Right Panel

With afghan hook and B, ch 96.
Rows 1–3: Work 3 rows of afghan st, change to MC in last st of last row: 96 sts.
Note: Read **Side Panel Chart** from left to right.
Rows 4–73: Foll **Side Panel Chart** on page 68: 97 sts.
Rows 74–257: Rep rows 28–73, 4 times.
Rows 258–285: Foll **Side Panel Chart.**
Row 286: Sl st in ea vertical bar across; fasten off.

Assembly

With rs facing and using MC, whip-stitch panels tog.

Border

Rnd 1 (ws): With ws facing and using crochet hook, join MC in back of 3rd st of row 3 with sl st, ch 1, sc in same st and in ea st across to corner, * 3 sc in corner, sc in ea st across to next corner; rep from * around; join with sl st to beg sc.
Rnds 2 and 3: Ch 1, sc back of next st of next row, sc in ea st across to corner, * 3 sc in corner; sc in ea st across to next corner; rep from * around; join with sl st to beg sc.
Rnd 4: Ch 1, sc in next sc and in ea sc across to corner, * 3 sc in corner; sc in ea st across to next corner; rep from * around; join with sl st to beg sc.

Afghan by Barbara Pawelko
Mt. Prospect, Illinois

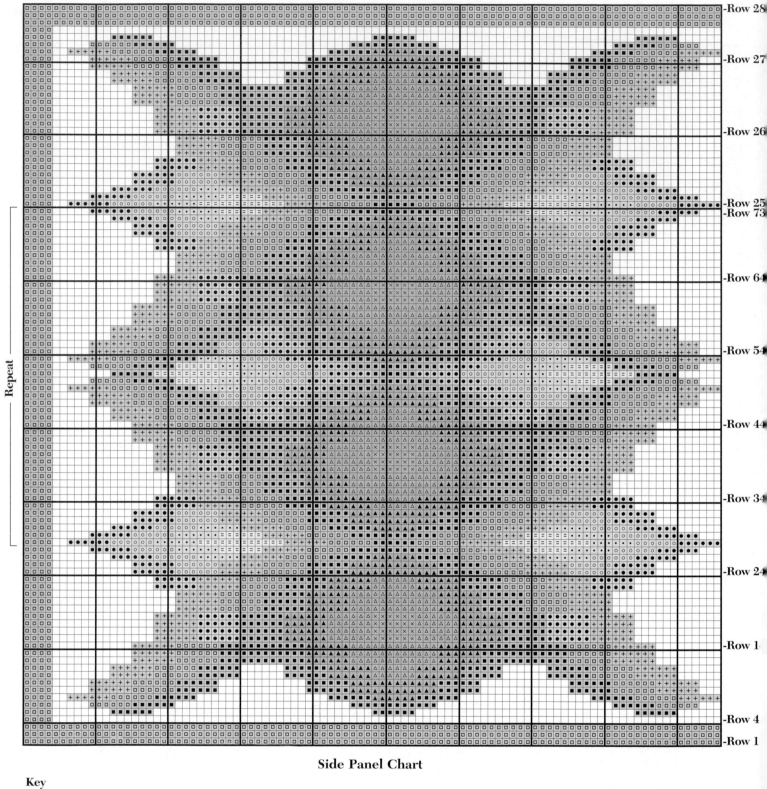

Side Panel Chart

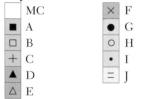

Key

☐	MC	✕	F	
■	A	●	G	
☐	B	○	H	
+	C	·	I	
▲	D	=	J	
△	E			

Note: Read ***Side Panel Chart*** from right to left for Left Panel and from left to right for Right Panel. If necessary, make reverse photocopy of ***Side Panel Chart.***

68

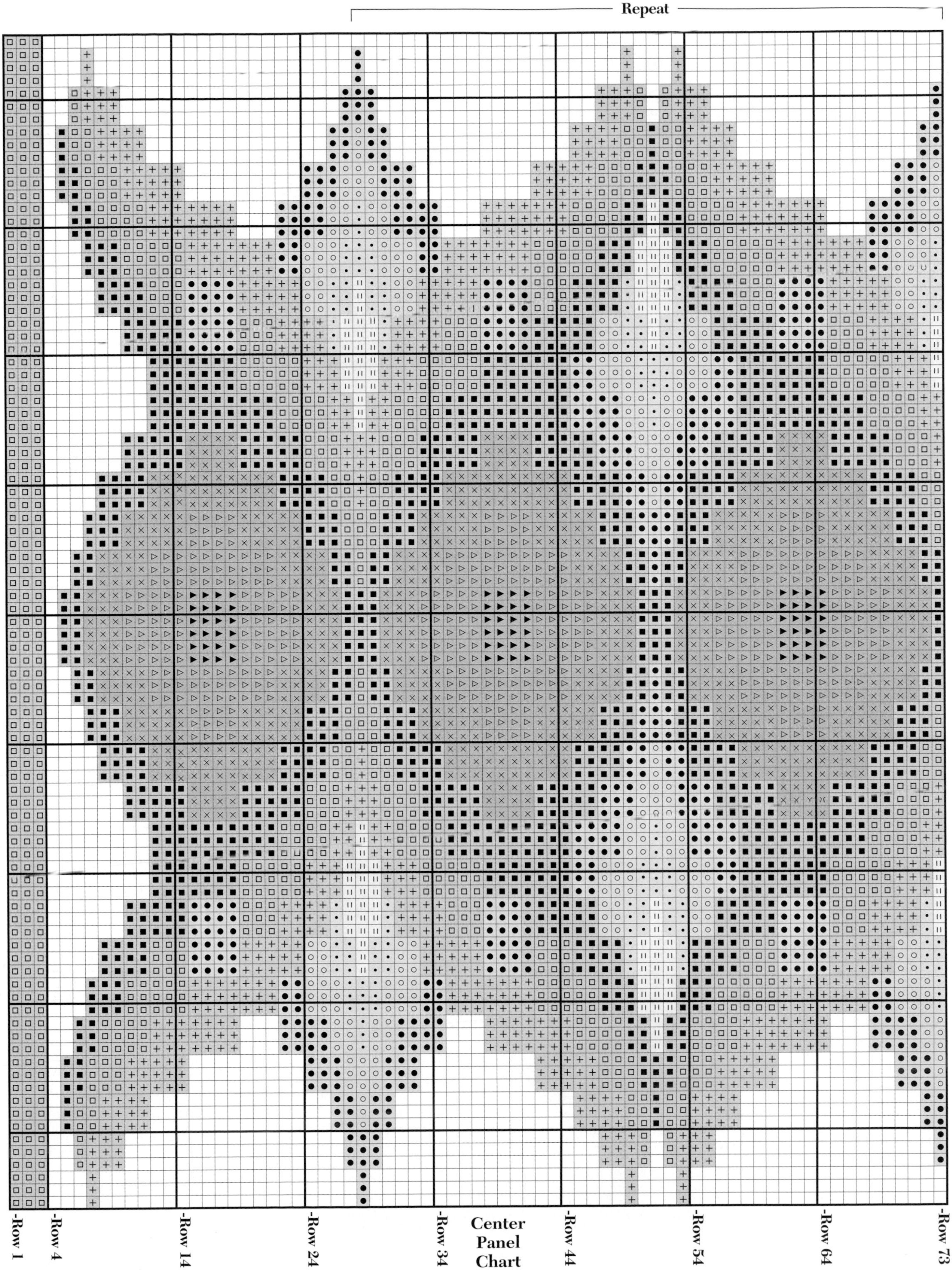

Center
Panel
Chart

-Row 1 -Row 4 -Row 14 -Row 24 -Row 34 -Row 44 -Row 54 -Row 64 -Row 73

Repeat

Christmas Celebration

Each panel contains a traditional symbol of the season. Easy embroidery and braided fringe are festive accents.

Worsted-weight acrylic yarn, approximately:
21 oz. (1,320 yd.) green, MC
14 oz. (880 yd.) white, A
17½ oz. (1,100 yd.) red, B
14 oz. (880 yd.) gold, C
Size I afghan hook or size to obtain gauge
Yarn needle

Finished Size

Approximately 50" x 60", without fringe

Gauge

13 sts and 11 rows = 3"

Note: See page 148 for afghan st directions.

Tree Panel (Make 3.)

With afghan hook and MC, ch 24.
Rows 1–4: Work 4 rows of afghan st: 24 sts.
Row 5: Step 1: Work same as Step 1 of afghan st. **Step 2:** Referring to *Tree Chart* on page 72, yo and pull through first lp on hook, (yo and pull through 2 lps on hook) 11 times, ch 3 [picot made], (yo and pull through 2 lps on hook) 12 times.
Rows 6–22: Cont foll *Tree Chart* as est.
Rows 23–220: Rep rows 5–22, 11 times.
Row 221: Work 1 row of afghan st: 24 sts.
Row 222: Sl st in ea vertical bar across; fasten off.

Snowflake Panel (Make 2.)

With afghan hook and A, ch 24.
Rows 1–3: Work 3 rows of afghan st: 24 sts.
Row 4: Step 1: Work same as Step 1 of afghan st. **Step 2:** Referring to *Snowflake Chart* on page 72, yo and pull through first lp on hook, (yo and pull through 2 lps on hook) 11 times, ch 3 [picot made], (yo and pull through 2 lps on hook) 12 times.
Rows 5–21: Cont foll *Snowflake Chart* as est.
Rows 22–219: Rep rows 4–21, 11 times.
Rows 220 and 221: Work 2 rows of afghan st: 24 sts.
Row 222: Sl st in ea vertical bar across; fasten off.

Candy Cane Panel (Make 2.)

With afghan hook and B, ch 24.
Rows 1–4: Work 4 rows of afghan st: 24 sts.
Row 5: Step 1: Work same as Step 1 of afghan st. **Step 2:** Referring to *Candy Cane Chart* on page 72, yo and pull through first lp on hook, (yo and pull through 2 lps on hook) 6 times, ch 3 [picot made], (yo and pull through 2 lps on hook) 17 times.
Rows 6–22: Cont foll *Candy Cane Chart* as est.
Rows 23–220: Rep rows 5–22, 11 times.
Row 221: Work 1 row of afghan st: 24 sts.
Row 222: Sl st in ea vertical bar across; fasten off.

Star Panel (Make 2.)

With afghan hook and C, ch 24.
Rows 1–4: Work 4 rows of afghan st: 24 sts.
Row 5: Step 1: Work same as

(continued)

Row 222: Sl st in ea vertical bar across; fasten off.

Assembly
With rs facing, whipstitch panels tog in foll sequence: * Tree Panel, Snowflake Panel, Candy Cane Panel, Star Panel; rep from * once, Tree Panel.

Embroidery
Referring to detail photos on page 70 and at left, straightstitch designs along seams.

Fringe
For ea tassel, referring to page 159 of General Directions, cut 2 (22") lengths of yarn. Working across short ends and matching colors, knot 1 tassel in every other st. Gather 4 tassels tog and divide strands into 2 grps of 5 and 1 grp of 6; braid grps, leaving 3" tails; knot tails tog and trim ends.

Afghan by Junella Latona Clovis, California

Step 1 of afghan st. **Step 2:** Referring to **Star Chart,** yo and pull through first lp on hook, (yo and pull through 2 lps on hook) 7 times, * ch 3 [picot made], (yo and pull through 2 lps on hook) 8 times; rep from * once.

Rows 6–22: Cont foll **Star Chart** as est.
Rows 23–220: Rep rows 5–22, 11 times.
Row 221: Work 1 row of afghan st: 24 sts.

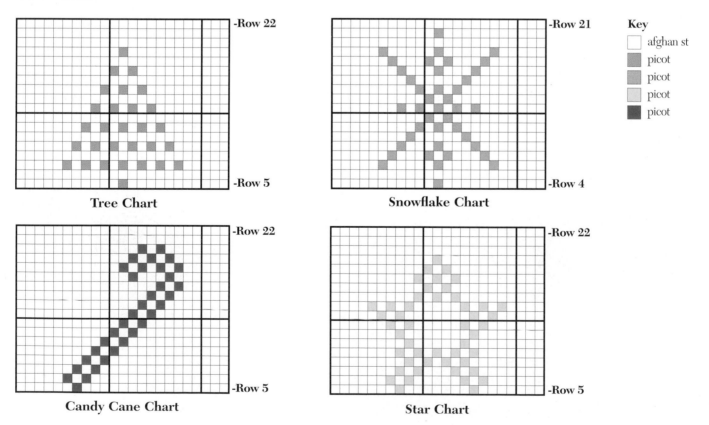

Tree Chart

Snowflake Chart

Candy Cane Chart

Star Chart

Key
afghan st
picot
picot
picot
picot

Hearts and Flowers

Knit a romantic throw with subtly textured hearts. Add stripes and flowers with simple duplicate stitch.

Materials

Worsted-weight acrylic yarn, approximately:
40 oz. (2,260 yd.) white, MC
3½ oz. (200 yd.) blue, A
Sportweight acrylic yarn, approximately:
2 oz. (200 yd.) dark rose, B
2 oz. (200 yd.) light rose, C
2 oz. (200 yd.) green, D
Size 8 circular knitting needles or size to obtain gauge
Size H crochet hook or size to obtain gauge
Yarn needle

Finished Size

Approximately 53" x 54"

Gauge

16 sts and 24 rows = 4"

With MC, CO 210 sts.

Rows 1–8: Work in St st for 8 rows.

Row 9 (rs): K 41, (p 2, k 40) 3 times, p 2, k 41.

Row 10 (ws): P 40, (k 4, p 38) 3 times, k 4, p 40.

Row 11: K 39, (p 2, k 2, p 2, k 36) 3 times, p 2, k 2, p 2, k 39.

Row 12: P 38, (k 2, p 4, k 2, p 34) 3 times, k 2, p 4, k 2, p 38.

Row 13: K 37, (p 2, k 6, p 2, k 32) 3 times, p 2, k 6, p 2, k 37.

Row 14: P 36, (k 2, p 8, k 2, p 30) 3 times, k 2, p 8, k 2, p 36.

Row 15: K 35, (p 2, k 10, p 2, k 28) 3 times, p 2, k 10, p 2, k 35.

Row 16: P 35, (k 2, p 10, k 2, p 28) 3 times, k 2, p 10, k 2, p 35.

Row 17: K 35, (p 2, k 4, p 2, k 4, p 2, k 28) 3 times, p 2, k 4, p 2, k 4, p 2, k 35.

Row 18: P 36, (k 2, p 2, k 4, p 2, k 2, p 30) 3 times, k 2, p 2, k 4, p 2, k 2, p 36.

Row 19: K 37, (p 4, k 2, p 4, k 32) 3 times, p 4, k 2, p 4, k 37.

Row 20: P 38, (k 2, p 4, k 2, p 34) 3 times, k 2, p 4, k 2, p 38.

Rows 21–36: Work in St st for 16 rows.

Row 37: K 20, (p 2, k 40) 4 times, p 2, k 20.

Row 38: P 19, (k 4, p 38) 4 times, k 4, p 19.

Row 39: K 18, (p 2, k 2, p 2, k 36) 4 times, p 2, k 2, p 2, k 18.

Row 40: P 17, (k 2, p 4, k 2, p 34) 4 times, k 2, p 4, k 2, p 17.

Row 41: K 16, (p 2, k 6, p 2, k 32) 4 times, p 2, k 6, p 2, k 16.

Row 42: P 15, (k 2, p 8, k 2, p 30) 4 times, k 2, p 8, k 2, p 15.

Row 43: K 14, (p 2, k 10, p 2, k 28) 4 times, p 2, k 10, p 2, k 14.

Row 44: P 14, (k 2, p 10, k 2, p 28) 4 times, k 2, p 10, k 2, p 14.

Row 45: K 14, (p 2, k 4, p 2, k 4, p 2, k 28) 4 times, p 2, k 4, p 2, k 4, p 2, k 14.

Row 46: P 15, (k 2, p 2, k 4, p 2, k 2, p 30) 4 times, k 2, p 2, k 4, p 2, k 2, p 15.

Row 47: K 16, (p 4, k 2, p 4, k 32) 4 times, p 4, k 2, p 4, k 16.

Row 48: P 17, (k 2, p 4, k 2, p 34) 4 times, k 2, p 4, k 2, p 17.

Rows 49–64: Work in St st for 16 rows.

Rows 65–356: Rep rows 9–64, 5 times, then rep rows 9–28 once; BO.

Duplicate Stitch

Referring to page 158 of General Directions and foll **Chart,** duplicate stitch stripes and flowers.

Border

With rs facing and crochet hook, join MC in any corner with sl st, ch 1, * (sc, ch 3, 2 dc) in next st, sl st in next st; rep from * around; fasten off.

Afghan by Diane O'Brien Minden, Nevada

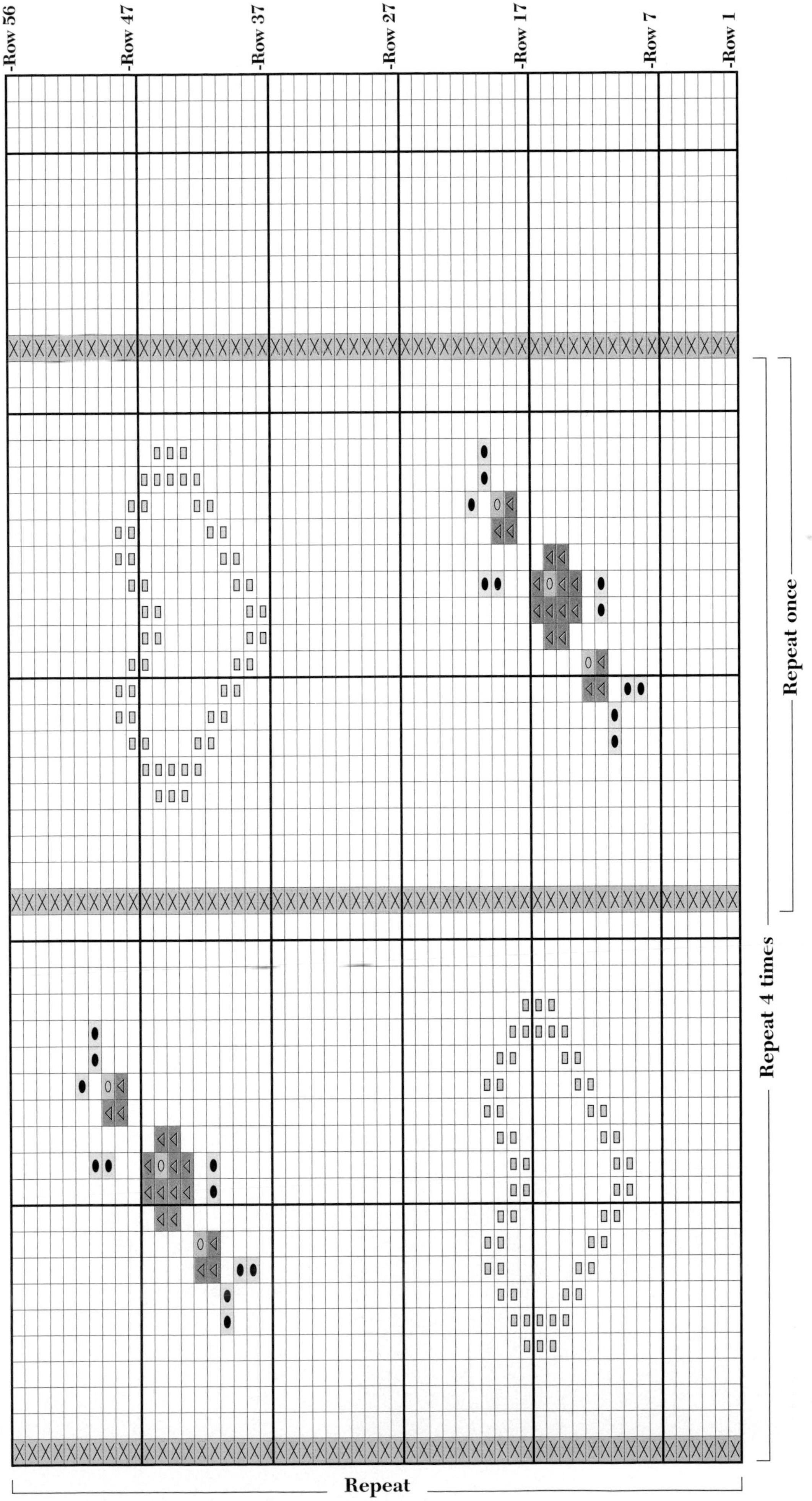

-Row 56 -Row 47 -Row 37 -Row 27 -Row 17 -Row 7 -Row 1

Key

MC-k	
MC-p	
A	×
B	△
C	○
D	●

Repeat once

Repeat 4 times

Repeat

Borderline

This striking design showcases an afghan-stitch variation that results in subtle texture.

Materials

Worsted-weight acrylic yarn, approximately:

21 oz. (1,170 yd.) tan, MC
28 oz. (1,560 yd.) navy, A
7 oz. (390 yd.) fuchsia, B
7 oz. (390 yd.) brown, C
14 oz. (780 yd.) teal, D
Size H afghan hook or size to
    obtain gauge
Size H crochet hook or size to
    obtain gauge
Yarn needle

Finished Size

Approximately 46" x 60"

Gauge

27 sts and 20 rows = 5"

Pattern Stitch

Purl: Holding yarn in front of work, insert hook in vertical bar indicated, yo and pull up lp.

Note: Work *texture pat* as folls:
Row 1: Work 1 row of afghan st.
Row 2: Step 1: Purl in first vertical bar, (holding yarn in back of work, pull up lp in afghan st, purl in next st) across. **Step 2:** Yo and pull through 1 lp, (yo and pull through 2 lps) across.
Row 3: Step 1: (Pull up 1 lp in afghan st, purl in next st) across.
Step 2: Yo and pull through 1 lp, (yo and pull through 2 lps) across.
    Rep rows 2 and 3 alternately.

Note: See page 148 for afghan st directions. To change colors in afghan st: **Step 1:** Drop yarn to ws of work, insert hook under next vertical bar and pull up lp with new color. Do not carry yarn over more than 3 sts. **Step 2:** Yo and pull through 2 lps on hook until 1 lp of current color rem on hook, drop yarn to ws of work, pick up new color, yo and pull through 2 lps on hook.

Left Panel

With afghan hook and A, ch 64.
Rows 1–5: Work 5 rows of afghan st: 64 sts.
Note: Read **Side Panel Chart** from right to left.
Rows 6–11: Cont foll **Side Panel Chart** on page 79: 64 sts.
Rows 12–16: Cont foll **Side Panel Chart,** work 21 sts in texture pat, work next 7 sts in afghan st, work next 21 sts in texture pat, work rem sts in afghan st: 64 sts.
Rows 17–46: Cont foll **Side Panel Chart:** 64 sts.
Rows 47–226: Rep rows 17–46, 6 times.
Rows 227–237: Cont foll **Side Panel Chart:** 64 sts.
Row 238: Sl st in ea vertical bar across; fasten off.

Right Panel

With afghan hook and A, ch 64.
Rows 1–5: Work 5 rows of afghan st: 64 sts.
Note: Read **Side Panel Chart** from left to right.
Rows 6–11: Cont foll **Side Panel Chart** on page 79: 64 sts.
Rows 12–16: Cont foll **Side Panel Chart,** work 15 sts in afghan st, work next 21 sts in texture pat, work next 7 sts in afghan st, work next 21 sts in texture pat: 64 sts.
Rows 17–46: Cont foll **Side Panel Chart:** 64 sts.
Rows 47–226: Rep rows 17–46, 6 times.
Rows 227–237: Cont foll **Side Panel Chart:** 64 sts.
Row 238: Sl st in ea vertical bar across; fasten off.

(continued)

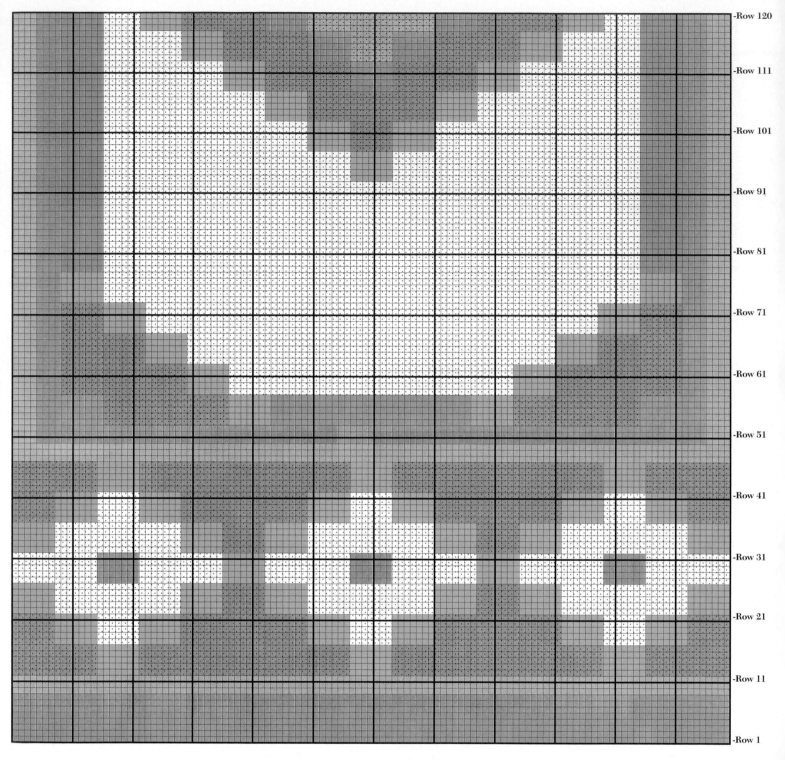

Center Panel Chart

Key

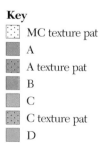

- MC texture pat
- A
- A texture pat
- B
- C
- C texture pat
- D

Center Panel

With afghan hook and A, ch 119.

Rows 1–5: Work 5 rows of afghan st: 64 sts.

Note: Read *Center Panel Chart* from right to left.

Rows 6–11: Cont foll *Center Panel Chart:* 119 sts.

Rows 12–16: Cont foll *Center Panel Chart,* work 14 sts in texture pat, (work next 7 sts in afghan st, work next 35 sts in texture pat) twice, work next 7 sts in afghan st, work last 14 sts in texture pat: 119 sts.

Rows 17–120: Cont foll *Center Panel Chart:* 119 sts.

Note: Turn *Chart* upside down and cont to read from right to left for rows 121–237 .

Rows 121–237: Reading *Center Panel Chart* upside down, rep rows 119–1, once: 119 sts.

Row 238: Sl st in ea vertical bar across; fasten off.

Assembly

With rs facing, whipstitch panels tog.

Outlines

Rnd 1: With rs facing, join MC in 15th st of row 12 with sl st, sl st across to 15th st of row 227, sl st across to last 15 sts of row 227, sl st across to last 15 sts of row 12, sl st across to beg sl st; join with sl st to beg sl st; fasten off.

Rnd 2: With rs facing, join MC in last st of row 47 of Center Panel with sl st, sl st across to last st of row 191 of Center Panel; sl st across to first st of row 191, sl st across to first st on row 47, sl st across to beg sl st; join with sl st to beg sl st; fasten off.

Border

With rs facing, join A in top right corner with sl st, working in bk lps only, sl st in ea st around; join with sl st to beg sc; fasten off.

Afghan by Barbara Pawelko
Mt. Prospect, Illinois

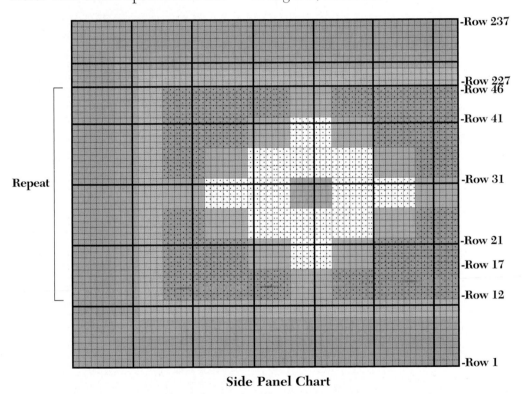

Side Panel Chart

Note: Read *Side Panel Chart* from right to left for Left Panel and from left to right for Right Panel. If necessary, make reverse photocopy of *Side Panel Chart.*

Lattice

Form this bold pattern by working row upon row of Xs.
Simply repeat the easy chart.

Materials

Worsted-weight acrylic yarn,
approximately:
40 oz. (2,260 yd.) burgundy,
   MC
24 oz. (1,360 yd.) navy, CC
Size I crochet hook or size to
   obtain gauge

Finished Size

Approximately 49" x 63"

Gauge

12 sc and 15 rows = 4"

Note: To change colors, work last yo
of prev st with new color, dropping
prev color to ws of work. Do not
carry yarn across row. Use 10 small
balls or bobbins of CC to work in
vertical zigzag. At Xs, work 2 sc from
1 bobbin and 2 sc from another
bobbin to cont working in vertical
zigzag. Use 11 small balls or bobbins
of MC.

With CC, ch 141.
Row 1 (ws): Referring to *Chart,*
sc in 2nd ch from hook and in next ch,
* change to MC, sc in next 24 chs,
change to CC, sc in next 2 chs **,

change to CC [next bobbin], sc in
next 2 chs; rep from * across, ending
last rep at **: 140 sc.
Rows 2–28: Cont foll **Chart** as est.
Rows 29–224: Rep rows 2–29, 7
times; fasten off.

Border

Rnd 1 (rs): With rs facing, join CC
in top right corner with sl st, ch 1,
* sc evenly across to next corner,
3 sc in corner; rep from * around;
join with sl st to beg sc; fasten off.
Rnd 2 (rs): With rs facing, join MC
in top right corner with sl st, ch 2,
* hdc evenly across to next corner,
3 hdc in corner; rep from * around;
join with sl st to top of beg ch-2;
fasten off.
Rnd 3 (rs): With rs facing, join MC
in top right corner with sl st, ch 1,
* sc evenly across to next corner,
3 sc in corner; rep from * around;
join with sl st to top of beg sc; fasten
off.

Afghan by Lois Miller
Monroe, Wisconsin

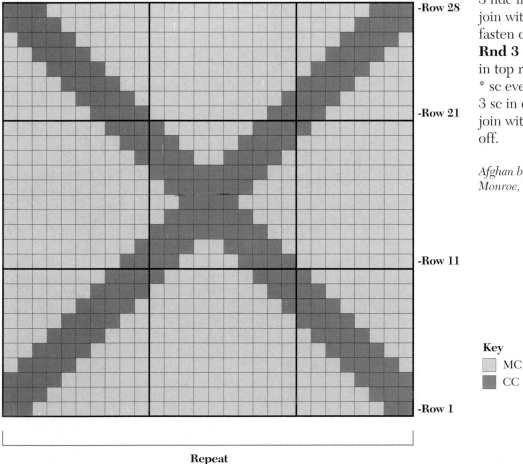

-Row 28

-Row 21

-Row 11

-Row 1

Key
- MC
- CC

Repeat

Chart

Bright Ribbons

Begin with a mesh background and then add ribbons of color over the mesh by working single crochet stitches in squiggly squares.

Materials

Worsted-weight acrylic yarn, approximately:
45 oz. (2,250 yd.) white, MC
18 oz. (900 yd.) red, A
15 oz. (750 yd.) green, B
Size G crochet hook or size to obtain gauge

Finished Size

Approximately 49" x 58", without fringe

Gauge

In pat, 6 dc and 5 rows = 3"

Mesh

With MC, ch 194.

Row 1 (rs): Dc in 6th ch from hook, * ch 1, sk next ch, dc in next ch; rep from * across: 95 ch-1 sps.

Rows 2–95: Ch 4 [counts as first dc plus ch 1], turn; dc in next dc, (ch 1, dc in next dc) across; fasten off after last row.

Ribbon Border

Rnd 1 (rs): With rs facing, join A in top right corner with sl st, ch 1, 2 sc in same corner, 2 sc around next dc, 2 sc in next ch-1 sp 1 row below, (2 sc around next dc, 2 sc in next ch-1 sp, 2 sc around next dc, 2 sc in next ch-1 sp 1 row below) across to last 2 dc, 2 dc around next dc, 4 sc in corner, (2 sc in ch-1 sp 1 row below, 2 sc around 2nd dc 1 row below, 2 sc in ch-1 sp 1 row below, 2 sc around first dc 1 row below) across to next corner, 2 sc in same corner, (2 sc around next dc, 2 sc in next ch-1 sp 1 row above, 2 sc around next dc, 2 sc in next ch-1 sp) across to last 2 dc, 2 dc around next dc,

4 sc in corner, (2 sc in ch-1 sp 1 row above, 2 sc around 2nd dc 1 row above, 2 sc in ch-1 sp 1 row above, 2 sc around first dc 1 row above) across to next corner; join with sl st to beg sc; fasten off.

Rnd 2 (rs): With rs facing, join A in 3rd ch-1 sp from right on row 3 with sl st, ch 1, 2 sc in same sp, working vertically, (2 sc around next dc 1 row above, 2 sc in ch-1 sp 1 row above, 2 sc around last dc 1 row above, 2 sc in ch-1 sp 1 row above) 45 times, working horizontally, (2 sc around next dc, 2 sc in ch-1 sp 1 row below, 2 sc around next dc, 2 sc in ch-1 sp) 45 times, 2 sc around next dc, working vertically, (2 sc in ch-1 sp 1 row below, 2 sc around last dc 1 row below, 2 sc in ch-1 sp 1 row below, 2 sc around next dc) 45 times, working horizontally, (2 sc in ch-1 sp 1 row below, 2 sc around next dc, 2 sc in next ch-1 sp, 2 sc around next dc) 45 times, 2 sc in ch-1 sp 1 row below, 2 sc around next dc; join with sl st to beg sc; fasten off.

Rnd 3: With rs facing, join MC in 5th ch-1 sp from right on row 5 with sl st, work same as rnd 2, working reps 43 times.

Rnd 4: With rs facing, join MC in 7th ch-1 sp from right on row 7 with sl st, work same as rnd 2, working reps 41 times.

Ribbon Square 1

Rnd 1 (rs): With rs facing, join B in 9th ch-1 sp from right on row 9 with sl st, ch 1, 2 sc in same sp, working vertically, (2 sc around next dc 1 row above, 2 sc in ch-1 sp 1 row above, 2 sc around last dc 1 row above, 2 sc in ch-1 sp 1 row above) 7 times, working horizontally, (2 sc around next dc, 2 sc in ch-1 sp 1 row below,

2 sc around next dc, 2 sc in ch-1 sp) 7 times, 2 sc around next dc, working vertically, (2 sc in ch-1 sp 1 row below, 2 sc around last dc 1 row below, 2 sc in ch-1 sp 1 row below, 2 sc around next dc) 7 times, working horizontally, (2 sc in ch-1 sp 1 row below, 2 sc around next dc, 2 sc in next ch-1 sp, 2 sc around next dc) 7 times, 2 sc in ch-1 sp 1 row below, 2 sc around next dc; join with sl st to beg sc; fasten off.

Rnd 2: With rs facing, join B in 11th ch-1 sp from right on row 11 with sl st, work same as rnd 2, working reps 5 times.

Rnd 3: With rs facing, join B in 13th ch-1 sp from right on row 13 with sl st, work same as rnd 2, working reps 3 times.

Rnd 4: With rs facing, join B in 15th ch-1 sp from right on row 15 with sl st, work same as rnd 2, working reps once.

Ribbon Square 2

Rnd 1 (rs): With rs facing, join A in ch-1 sp next to Ribbon Square 1 with sl st, work same as rnd 1 of Ribbon Square 1.

Rnd 2: With A, work same as rnd 2 of Ribbon Square 1.

Rnds 3 and 4: With MC, work same as rnds 3 and 4 of Ribbon Square 1.

Cont working Ribbon Squares 1 and 2 in checkerboard fashion: 25 Ribbon Squares.

Fringe

For ea tassel, referring to page 159 of General Directions, cut 8 (14") lengths of yarn. Working across short ends, knot 1 tassel in every other ch-1 sp.

Afghan by Monica Kancel-Costello Hannibal, Ohio

Cheyenne Chevron

You'll find chevron motifs in many Native American arts.
Work this afghan sideways with the right side always facing
so that the yarn tails become the fringe.

Materials

Worsted-weight acrylic yarn,
   approximately:
30 oz. (1,500 yd.) cream, MC
12 oz. (600 yd.) brown, A
9 oz. (450 yd.) tan, B
9 oz. (450 yd.) red, C
Size H crochet hook or size to
   obtain gauge

Finished Size

Approximately 57" x 63", without
fringe

Gauge

14 sc and 13 rows = 4"

Note: Afghan is worked sideways. All
rows are worked with rs facing.
Leave 6" tail at beg and end of ea
row for fringe.

Pattern Stitch

Ldc: Dc in ft lp of next st 1 row
below.

With A, ch 219; fasten off.
Row 1 (rs): With rs facing, join A in
first ch with sl st, ch 1, sc in same ch
and in ea ch across; fasten off: 219 sc.
Rows 2–4: Join A in first sc with
sl st, ch 1, sc in same sc and in next
4 sc; working in bk lps only, sc in ea
sc across to last 5 sc; working in both
lps, sc in last 5 sc; fasten off: 219 sc.
Rows 5 and 6: With MC, rep row 2
twice.
Row 7: Join MC in first sc with sl st,
ch 1, sc in same sc and in next 4 sc,
Ldc, (working in bk lps only, sc in
next 10 sts, Ldc) 18 times; working
in bk lps only, sc in next 11 sts;
working in both lps, sc in last 5 sc;
fasten off: 19 dc.
Row 8: Join MC in first sc with sl st,
ch 1, sc in same sc and in next 4 sc;
working in bk lps only, sc in next st,
Ldc, (sc in next 10 sts, Ldc) 18 times,
sc in next 9 sts; working in both lps,
sc in last 5 sc; fasten off: 19 dc.
Row 9: Join MC in first sc with sl st,
ch 1, sc in same sc and in next 4 sc;
working in bk lps only, sc in next
2 sts, Ldc, (sc in next 10 sts, Ldc) 18
times, sc in next 8 sts; working in
both lps, sc in last 5 sc; fasten off:
19 dc.
Row 10: Join MC in first sc with sl st,
ch 1, sc in same sc and in next 4 sc;
working in bk lps only, sc in next
3 sts, Ldc, (sc in next 10 sts, Ldc) 18
times, sc in next 7 sts; working in both
lps, sc in last 5 sc; fasten off: 19 dc.
Row 11: Join MC in first sc with sl st,
ch 1, sc in same sc and in next 4 sc;
working in bk lps only, sc in next
4 sts, Ldc, (sc in next 10 sts, Ldc) 18
times, sc in next 6 sts; working in both
lps, sc in last 5 sc; fasten off: 19 dc.
Row 12: Join MC in first sc with sl st,
ch 1, sc in same sc and in next 4 sc;
working in bk lps only, sc in next
5 sts, Ldc, (sc in next 10 sts, Ldc) 18
times, sc in next 5 sts; working in both
lps, sc in last 5 sc; fasten off: 19 dc.
Row 13: Join MC in first sc with sl st,
ch 1, sc in same sc and in next 4 sc;
working in bk lps only, sc in next
6 sts, Ldc, (sc in next 10 sts, Ldc) 18
times, sc in next 4 sts; working in both
lps, sc in last 5 sc; fasten off: 19 dc.
Row 14: Join MC in first sc with sl st,
ch 1, sc in same sc and in next 4 sc;
working in bk lps only, sc in next
7 sts, Ldc, (sc in next 10 sts, Ldc) 18
times, sc in next 3 sts; working in both
lps, sc in last 5 sc; fasten off: 19 dc.
Row 15: Join MC in first sc with sl st,
ch 1, sc in same sc and in next 4 sc;
working in bk lps only, sc in next
8 sts, Ldc, (sc in next 10 sts, Ldc) 18
times, sc in next 2 sts; working in both
lps, sc in last 5 sc; fasten off: 19 dc.
Row 16: Join MC in first sc with
sl st, ch 1, sc in same sc and in next
4 sc; working in bk lps only, sc in
next 9 sts, Ldc, (sc in next 10 sts,
Ldc) 18 times, sc in next st; working
in both lps, sc in last 5 sc; fasten off:
19 dc.
Row 17: Rep row 15.
Row 18: Rep row 14.
Row 19: Rep row 13.
Row 20: Rep row 12.
Row 21: Rep row 11.
Row 22: Rep row 10.
Row 23: Rep row 9.
Row 24: Rep row 8.
Row 25: Rep row 7.
Rows 26–34: Rep rows 8–16,
changing colors in foll sequence:
3 rows ea of A, B, and C.
Row 35: Join A in first sc with sl st,
ch 1, sc in same sc and in next 4 sc,
working in bk lps only, sc in next
10 sts, Ldc, (sc in next 10 sts, Ldc)
18 times, working in both lps, sc in
last 5 sc; fasten off: 19 dc.
Rows 36–44: Rep rows 16–24,
changing colors in the foll sequence:
3 rows ea of C, B, and A.
Rows 45–177: Rep rows 7–44, 3
times, then rep rows 7–25 once.
Rows 178–181: Rep row 2, 4 times.

Fringe

For ea tassel, knot 4 tails tog.

Afghan by Joy Bowlin
Santee, California

Pretty in Pink

Bubble-gum pink post stitches make this oversize
afghan extra thick and warm.

Materials
Worsted-weight acrylic yarn,
approximately:
88 oz. (4,975 yd.) pink
Size J crochet hook or size to
obtain gauge

Finished Size
Approximately 57" x 74"

Gauge
In pat, 13 dc and 8 rows = 4"

Pattern Stitches
FPdc: Yo, insert hook from front to
back around st indicated, yo and pull
up lp, (yo and pull through 2 lps)
twice.
BPdc: Yo, insert hook from back to
front around st indicated, yo and
pull up lp, (yo and pull through
2 lps) twice.

Ch 182.
Row 1: Sc in 2nd ch from hook and
in ea ch across: 181 sc.
Rows 2–10: Ch 1, turn; working in
bk lps only, sc in first sc and in ea sc
across: 181 sc.
Row 11: Ch 2 [counts as first hdc
throughout], turn; working in bk lps
only, hdc in next 9 sts; working in
both lps, hdc in ea st across to last
10 sts; working in bk lps only, hdc in
last 10 sts: 181 hdc.
Row 12: Ch 2, turn; working in
bk lps only, hdc in next 9 sts,
(FPdc around next st, BPdc around
next st) across to last 10 sts; working
in bk lps only, hdc in last 10 sts.
Rows 13 and 14: Ch 2, turn; working in bk lps only, hdc in next 9 sts,
(BPdc around next st, FPdc around
next st) across to last 10 sts; working
in bk lps only, hdc in last 10 sts.
Row 15: Rep row 12.
Rep rows 12–15 until piece measures approximately 71"; then rep
row 11 once; then rep row 2, 10
times; fasten off.

*Afghan by Claudia Quattlebaum
Bowman, South Carolina*

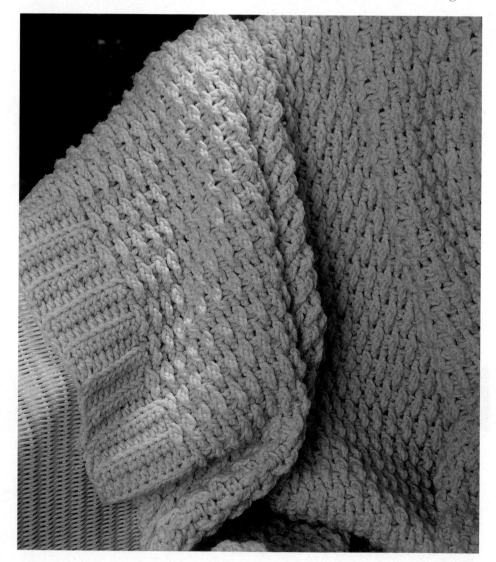

Hummingbirds

Three charming birds hover near a column of bright pink flowers.
Follow the charts to make this lovely scene.

Materials

Worsted-weight acrylic yarn, approximately:
56 oz. (3,165 yd.) cream, MC
3½ oz. (200 yd.) dark gray, A
3½ oz. (200 yd.) sage green, B
3½ oz. (200 yd.) hot pink, C
3½ oz. (200 yd.) pale rose, D
1¾ oz. (100 yd.) yellow, E
1¾ oz. (100 yd.) fuchsia, F
1¾ oz. (100 yd.) pine green, G
7 oz. (400 yd.) light gray, H
1¾ oz. (100 yd.) white, I
1¾ oz. (100 yd.) black, J
Size I afghan hook or size to
    obtain gauge
Size I crochet hook or size to
    obtain gauge
Yarn needle

Finished Size

Approximately 52" x 63", without fringe

Gauge

In afghan st, 14 sts and 13 rows = 4"

Note: See page 148 for afghan st directions. To change colors in afghan st: **Step 1:** Drop yarn to ws of work, insert hook under next vertical bar and pull up lp with new color. Do not carry yarn over more than 3 sts. **Step 2:** Yo and pull through 2 lps on hook until 1 lp of current color rem on hook, drop yarn to ws of work, pick up new color, yo and pull through 2 lps on hook.

Hummingbird Panel

With afghan hook and MC, ch 100.
Rows 1–37: Work 37 rows of afghan st: 100 sts.
Rows 38–95: Foll **Hummingbird**

Chart A on page 90: 100 sts.
Rows 96–145: With MC, work 50 rows of afghan st: 100 sts.
Rows 146–174: Foll **Hummingbird Chart B** on page 91: 100 sts.
Rows 175–201: With MC, work 27 rows of afghan st: 100 sts.
Row 202: Sl st in ea vertical bar across; fasten off.
Edging
With rs facing and crochet hook, join MC in top left corner with sl st, ch 1, sc evenly across to next corner; fasten off.
Embroidery
Referring to page 159 of General Directions and **Hummingbird Charts,** make French knot eyes with H.

Flower Panel

With afghan hook and MC, ch 40.
Rows 1–101: Foll **Flower Chart** on page 91: 40 sts.
Rows 102–200: Rep rows 17–101 once, then rep rows 2–15 once: 40 sts.
Row 201: With MC, work 1 row of afghan st: 40 sts.
Row 202: Sl st in ea vertical bar across; fasten off.
Embroidery
Referring to page 159 of General Directions and **Flower Chart,** make French knots with E.
Edging
With rs facing and crochet hook, join MC in top left corner with sl st, ch 1, sc evenly across to next corner; fasten off. Rep along right edge of panel.

Plain Panel

With afghan hook and MC, ch 40.
Rows 1–201: With MC, work 201 rows of afghan st: 40 sts.

Row 202: Sl st in ea vertical bar across; fasten off.
Edging
With rs facing and crochet hook, join MC in bottom right corner with sl st, ch 1, sc evenly across to next corner; fasten off.

Assembly

With crochet hook, ws tog and working in bk lps only, sl st panels tog in foll sequence: Plain Panel, Flower Panel, Hummingbird Panel.
Stripe: With crochet hook, join MC to 8th vertical bar on row 1 with sl st, working vertically, sl st loosely in ea vertical bar across to top; fasten off.
  Rep Stripe beg in 10th vertical bar on row 1. Rep Stripe beg in 8th and 10th vertical bars on row 1 on opposite side of afghan.
  Rep Stripe beg 1 vertical bar from ea side of ea panel joining.

Border

With rs facing and crochet hook, join MC in top right corner with sl st, ch 1, 3 sc in same st, sc in ea st across to next corner, * 3 sc in corner, sc evenly across to next corner; rep from * around; join with sl st to bg sc; fasten off.

Fringe

For ea tassel, referring to page 159 of General Directions, cut 5 (20") lengths of MC. Working across short ends, knot 1 tassel in approximately every 3rd st.

Afghan by Dorothy Warrell
Granville, Ohio

Key

□	MC
+	A
●	B
▣	C
‖	D
✕	E
╱	F
○	G
╲	H
●	H (French knot)
=	I
■	J

Hummingbird Chart A

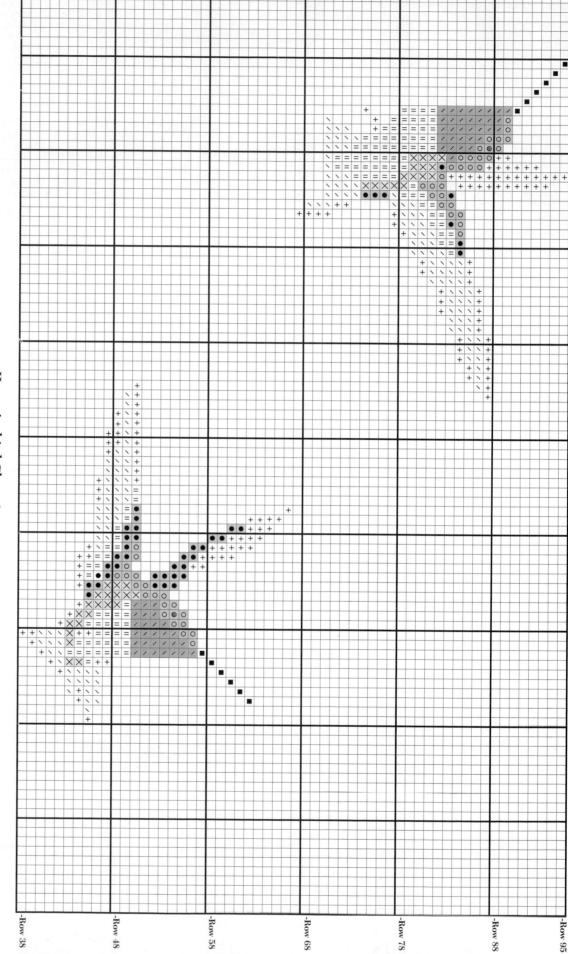

-Row 38   -Row 48   -Row 58   -Row 68   -Row 78   -Row 88   -Row 95

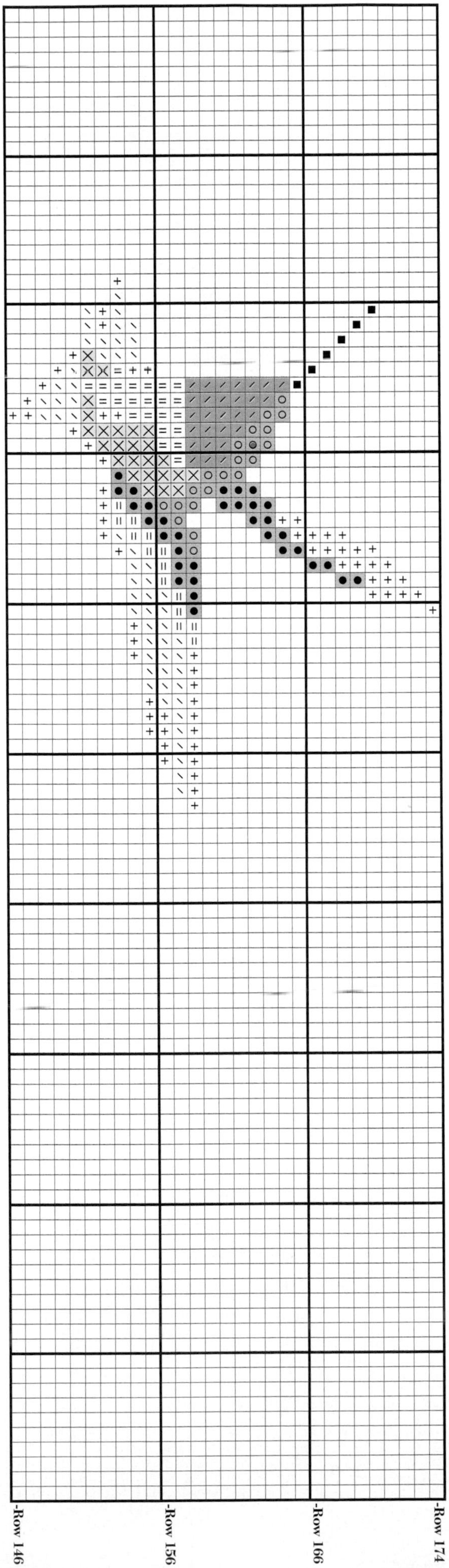

Hummingbird Chart B

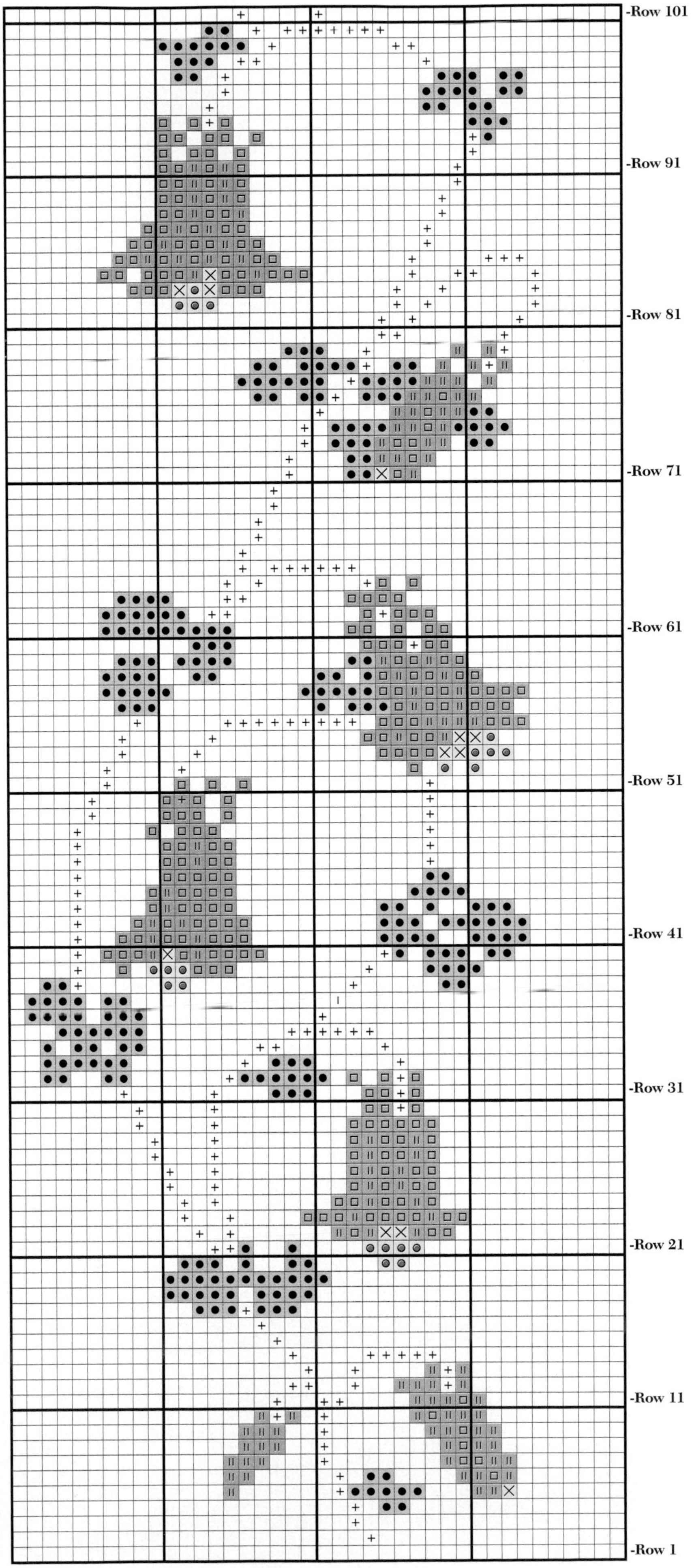

Flower Chart

-Row 101
-Row 91
-Row 81
-Row 71
-Row 61
-Row 51
-Row 41
-Row 31
-Row 21
-Row 11
-Row 1

-Row 146
-Row 156
-Row 166
-Row 174

Tumbling Blocks

Create a dimensional optical illusion with simple single crochet stitches and only three colors of yarn.

Materials

Worsted-weight acrylic yarn, approximately:
16 oz. (905 yd.) cream, MC
16 oz. (905 yd.) rose, A
16 oz. (905 yd.) blue, B
Size K crochet hook or size to obtain gauge

Finished Size

Approximately 42" x 64"

Gauge

15 sc and 18 rows = 5"

Note: To change colors, work last yo of prev st with new color, dropping prev color to ws of work. Do not carry yarn across row. Use separate balls or bobbins for ea color.

With MC, ch 121.
Row 1 (ws): Referring to **Chart**, * sc in 2nd ch from hook and in next 10 chs [11 sc], change to A, sc in next ch, change to B, sc in next ch, change to MC, sc in next 11 chs, rep from * across: 120 sc.
Rows 2–64: Cont foll **Chart** as est.
Rows 65–224: Rep rows 1–64 twice, then rep rows 1–32 once; do not fasten off MC.

Border

Rnd 1 (ws): Ch 1, turn; * sc evenly across to corner, 3 sc in corner; rep from * around; join with sl st to beg sc; fasten off.
Rnd 2 (rs): With rs facing, join B in top right corner with sl st, ch 1, sc in same st and in ea st across to corner, * 3 sc in corner, sc in ea st across to next corner; rep from * around; join with sl st to beg sc; fasten off.
Rnd 3 (ws): With ws facing, join A in top right corner with sl st, ch 1, sc in same st and in ea st across to corner, * 3 sc in corner, sc in ea st across to next corner; rep from * around; join with sl st to beg sc; fasten off.

Afghan by Lois Miller
Monroe, Wisconsin

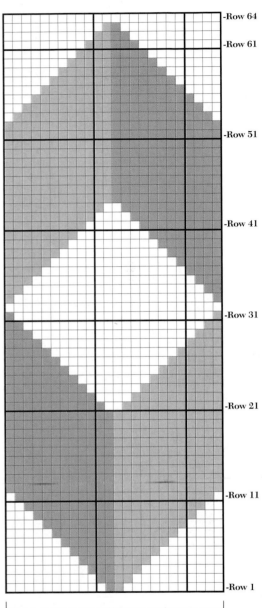

Row 64
Row 61
Row 51
Row 41
Row 31
Row 21
Row 11
Row 1

Repeat

Chart

Key
☐ MC
A
B

93

Cowboy Blues

Post stitches and puff stitches make a great cabled rope
pattern on this sturdy throw. When you're through,
try your hand at knotted fringe.

Materials

Worsted-weight acrylic yarn,
approximately:
72 oz. (4,070 yd.) blue
Size I crochet hook or size to
obtain gauge

Finished Size

Approximately 50" x 67", without
fringe

Gauge

13 dc and 7½ rows = 4"

Pattern Stitches

FPdc: Yo, insert hook from front to
back around st indicated, yo and pull
up lp, (yo and pull through 2 lps)
twice.

Dc/FPdc: Yo, insert hook in st indicated, yo and pull up lp, yo and pull
through 2 lps, yo, insert hook from
front to back around next st, yo and
pull up lp, yo and pull through 2 lps,
yo and pull through 3 lps.

FPdc/dc: Yo, insert hook from front
to back around st indicated, yo and
pull up lp, yo and pull through 2 lps,
yo, insert hook in next st, yo and pull
up lp, yo and pull through 2 lps,
yo and pull through 3 lps.

BPdc: Yo, insert hook from back to
front around st indicated, yo and
pull up lp, (yo and pull through
2 lps) twice.

Dc/BPdc: Yo, insert hook in st indicated, yo and pull up lp, yo and pull
through 2 lps, yo, insert hook from
back to front around next st, yo and
pull up lp, yo and pull through 2 lps,
yo and pull through 3 lps.

BPdc/dc: Yo, insert hook from back
to front around st indicated, yo and
pull up lp, yo and pull through 2 lps,
yo, insert hook in next st, yo and pull
up lp, yo and pull through 2 lps,
yo and pull through 3 lps.

Puff: (Yo, insert hook in st indicated,
yo and pull up lp) 4 times, yo and
pull through all 9 lps on hook, ch 1.

Dc-cl: Yo, insert hook in st indicated, yo and pull up lp, yo and pull
through 2 lps, yo, insert hook from
front to back around next st, yo and
pull up lp, yo and pull through 2 lps,
yo, insert hook in next st, yo and pull
up lp, yo and pull through 2 lps,
yo and pull through all 4 lps.

Tr-cl: * Yo twice, insert hook from
front to back around next st indicated, yo and pull up lp, (yo and pull
through 2 lps) twice **, yo, insert
hook from front to back around next
st, yo and pull up lp, yo and pull
through 2 lps; rep from * to ** once,
yo and pull through all 4 lps.

Ch 161.

Row 1 (ws): Dc in 4th ch from hook
and in ea ch across: 159 dc.
Row 2: Ch 3, turn; dc in next 2 sts,
* FPdc around next st, dc in next
2 sts, FPdc around next st, dc in next

(continued)

4 sts, dc/FPdc beg in next st, dc/FPdc beg in same st as last FPdc, dc in same st as last FPdc, (FPdc/dc beg around same st as last dc) twice, dc in next 4 sts, FPdc around next sts, dc in next 2 sts, FPdc around next st **, dc in next 3 sts, sk 2 sts, 5 dc in next st, ch 2, sk 3 sts, dc in next 3 sts; rep from * across, ending last rep at **, dc in last 3 sts.

Row 3: Ch 3, turn; dc in next 2 sts, * BPdc around next st, dc in next 2 sts, BPdc around next st, dc in next 3 sts, dc/BPdc beg in next st, dc/BPdc beg in same st as last BPdc, dc in same st as last BPdc, puff in next st, dc in next dc, (BPdc/dc beg around same st as last dc) twice, dc in next 3 dc, BPdc around next st, dc in next 2 sts, BPdc around next st, dc in next 3 sts **, sk ch-2 sp, 5 dc in next dc, ch 2, sk next 4 sts, dc in next 3 sts; rep from * across, ending last rep at **.

Row 4: Ch 3, turn; dc in next 2 sts, * FPdc around next st, dc in next 2 sts, FPdc around next st, dc in next 3 sts, FPdc around next 2 sts, dc in same st as last FPdc, dc-cl beg in next st, dc in next st, FPdc around same st and next st, dc in next 3 sts, FPdc around next st, dc in next 2 sts, FPdc around next st, dc in next 3 sts **, sk ch-2 sp, 5 dc in next dc, ch 2, sk next 4 sts, dc in next 3 sts; rep from * across, ending last rep at **.

Row 5: Ch 3, turn; dc in next 2 sts,

* BPdc around next st, dc in next 2 sts, BPdc around next st, dc in next 4 sts, (BPdc/dc beg around same st as last dc) twice, puff in next st, dc/BPdc beg in next dc, dc/BPdc beg in same st as last BPdc, dc in same st as last BPdc and in next 3 dc, BPdc around next st, dc in next 2 sts, BPdc around next st, dc in next 3 sts **, sk ch-2 sp, 5 dc in next dc, ch 2, sk next 4 sts, dc in next 3 sts; rep from * across, ending last rep at **.

Row 6: Ch 3, turn; dc in next 2 sts, * FPdc around next st, dc in next 2 sts, FPdc around next st, dc in next 5 sts, FPdc/dc beg around same st as last dc, tr-cl beg around last BPdc, dc/FPdc beg in same st as last FPtr, dc in same dc as last FPdc and in next 4 sts, FPdc around next st, dc in next 2 sts, FPdc around next st, dc in next 3 sts **, sk ch-2 sp, 5 dc in next dc, ch 2, sk next 4 sts, dc in next 3 sts; rep from * across, ending last rep at **.

Row 7: Ch 3, turn; dc in next 2 sts, * BPdc around next st, dc in next 2 sts, BPdc around next st, dc in next 13 sts, BPdc around next st, dc in next 2 sts, BPdc around next st, dc in next 3 sts **, sk ch-2 sp, 5 dc in next dc, ch 2, sk next 4 sts, dc in next 3 sts; rep from * across, ending last rep at **.

Row 8: Ch 3, turn; dc in next 2 sts, * FPdc around next st, dc in next

2 sts, FPdc around next st, dc in next 4 sts, dc/FPdc beg in next st, dc/FPdc beg in same st as last FPdc, dc in same st as last FPdc, (FPdc/dc beg around same st as last dc) twice, dc in next 4 sts, FPdc around next sts, dc in next 2 sts, FPdc around next st **, dc in next 3 sts, sk ch-2 sp, 5 dc in next st, ch 2, sk 4 sts, dc in next 3 sts; rep from * across, ending last rep at **, dc in last 3 sts.

Rows 9–127: Rep rows 3–8, 19 times, then rep rows 3–7 once; do not fasten off.

Edging

Row 1 (rs): Ch 3, turn; dc in next st and in ea st across.

Row 2: Ch 1, turn; sc in first dc, (ch 3, sk 1 dc, sc in next dc) across; fasten off.

Row 3 (rs): With rs facing, join yarn in bottom left corner with sl st, ch 3, dc in next st and in ea st across.

Row 4: Rep row 2.

Fringe

For ea tassel, referring to page 159 of General Directions, cut 4 (20") lengths of yarn. Working across short ends, knot 1 tassel in ea ch-3 sp. Double-knot fringe 3 times.

Afghan by Carla Kisielnicki
McKeesport, Pennsylvania

Colorful Cables

This knitted masterpiece will challenge the experienced knitter with lots of crossed cables. Be sure to keep your bobbins closely wound to avoid tangles.

Materials

Worsted-weight acrylic yarn, approximately:

28 oz. (1,680 yd.) navy, MC
3½ oz. (210 yd.) green, A
3½ oz. (210 yd.) light blue, B
3½ oz. (210 yd.) dark rose, C
3½ oz. (210 yd.) pink, D
Size 9 circular knitting needles or size to obtain gauge
Cable needle

Finished Size

Approximately 48" x 64"

Gauge

In pat, 20 sts and 22 rows = 4"

Pattern Stitches

Cable front (CF): Sl 2 colored sts onto cable needle as if to p, hold in front of work, with MC, k 1, with bobbin, k 2 from cable needle.

Cable back (CB): Sl 1 MC st onto cable needle as if to p, hold in back of work, with bobbin, k 2, with MC, k 1 from cable needle.

Left cross: Sl 2 colored sts onto cable needle as if to p, hold in front of work, with next bobbin, k 2, with prev bobbin, k 2 from cable needle.

Right cross: Sl 2 colored sts onto cable needle as if to p, hold in back of work, with next bobbin, k 2, with prev bobbin, k 2 from cable needle.

Note: Use 1 small ball or bobbin for ea cable.

With MC, CO 238 sts.
Rows 1–6: Work in seed st for 6 rows.
Row 7 (rs): (K 1, p 1) 4 times, k 1, * join A, k 2, change to MC, k 3, join B, k 2, change to MC, k 3, join C, k 2, change to MC, k 3, join D, k 2, change to MC, k 10, join D, k 2, change to MC, k 3, join C, k 2, change to MC, k 3, join B, k 2, change to MC, k 3, join A, k 2; rep from * 4 times, k 1, (k 1, p 1) 4 times.

Row 8 and All Even Rows through Row 342: (P 1, k 1) 4 times, p across to last 10 sts, changing colors to match prev row, (p 1, k 1) 4 times.
Row 9: (K 1, p 1) 4 times, k 1, * (CF, k 2) 3 times, CF, k 8, (CB, k 2) 3 times, CB; rep from * 4 times, k 1, (k 1, p 1) 4 times.
Row 11: (K 1, p 1) 4 times, k 2, * (CF, k 2) 3 times, CF, k 6, (CB, k 2) 3 times, CB, k 2; rep from * 4 times, (k 1, p 1) 4 times.
Row 13: (K 1, p 1) 4 times, k 3, * (CF, k 2) 3 times, CF, k 4, (CB, k 2) 3 times, CB **, k 4; rep from * 4 times, ending last rep at **, k 3, (k 1, p 1) 4 times.
Row 15: (K 1, p 1) 4 times, k 4, * (CF, k 2) 4 times, (CB, k 2) 3 times, CB **, k 6; rep from * 4 times, ending last rep at **, k 4, (k 1, p 1) 4 times.
Row 17: (K 1, p 1) 4 times, k 5, * (CF, k 2) 3 times, CF, (CB, k 2) 3 times, CB **, k 8; rep from * 4 times, ending last rep at **, k 5, (k 1, p 1) 4 times.
Row 19: (K 1, p 1) 4 times, k 6, * (CF, k 2) 3 times, right cross, (k 2, CB) 3 times **, k 10; rep from * 4 times, ending last rep at **, k 6, (k 1, p 1) 4 times.
Row 21: (K 1, p 1) 4 times, k 7, * (CF, k 2) twice, (CF, CB) twice, (k 2, CB) twice **, k 12; rep from * 4 times, ending last rep at **, k 7, (k 1, p 1) 4 times.
Row 23: (K 1, p 1) 4 times, k 8, * (CF, k 2) twice, (left cross, k 2) twice, CB, k 2, CB **, k 14; rep from * 4 times, ending last rep at **, k 8, (k 1, p 1) 4 times.
Row 25: (K 1, p 1) 4 times, k 9, * CF, k 2, (CF, CB) 3 times, k 2, CB **, k 16; rep from * 4 times, ending last rep at **, k 9, (k 1, p 1) 4 times.
Row 27: (K 1, p 1) 4 times, k 10, * CF, k 2, (right cross, k 2) 3 times, CB **, k 18; rep from * 4 times, ending last rep at **, k 10, (k 1, p 1) 4 times.

Row 29: (K 1, p 1) 4 times, k 11, * (CF, CB) 4 times **, k 20; rep from * 4 times, ending last rep at **, k 11, (k 1, p 1) 4 times.
Row 31: (K 1, p 1) 4 times, k 12, * (left cross, k 2) 3 times, left cross **, k 22; rep from * 4 times, ending last rep at **, k 12, (k 1, p 1) 4 times.
Row 33: (K 1, p 1) 4 times, k 11, * (CB, CF) 4 times **, k 20; rep from * 4 times, ending last rep at **, k 11, (k 1, p 1) 4 times.
Row 35: (K 1, p 1) 4 times, k 10, * CB, k 2, (right cross, k 2) 3 times, CF **, k 18; rep from * 4 times, ending last rep at **, k 10, (k 1, p 1) 4 times.
Row 37: (K 1, p 1) 4 times, k 9, * CB, k 2, (CB, CF) 3 times, k 2, CF **, k 16; rep from * 4 times, ending last rep at **, k 9, (k 1, p 1) 4 times.
Row 39: (K 1, p 1) 4 times, k 8, * (CB, k 2) twice, (left cross, k 2) twice, CF, k 2, CF **, k 14; rep from * 4 times, ending last rep at **, k 8, (k 1, p 1) 4 times.
Row 41: (K 1, p 1) 4 times, k 7, * (CB, k 2) twice, (CB, CF) twice, (k 2, CF) twice **, k 12; rep from * 4 times, ending last rep at **, k 7, (k 1, p 1) 4 times.
Row 43: (K 1, p 1) 4 times, k 6, * (CB, k 2) 3 times, right cross, k 2, (CF, k 2) twice, CF **, k 10; rep from * 4 times, ending last rep at **, k 6, (k 1, p 1) 4 times.
Row 45: (K 1, p 1) 4 times, k 5, * (CB, k 2) 3 times, CB, (CF, k 2) 3 times, CF **, k 8; rep from * 4 times, ending last rep at **, k 5, (k 1, p 1) 4 times.
Row 47: (K 1, p 1) 4 times, k 4, * (CB, k 2) 4 times, (CF, k 2) 3 times, CF **, k 6; rep from * 4 times, ending last rep at **, k 4, (k 1, p 1) 4 times.
Row 49: (K 1, p 1) 4 times, k 3, * (CB, k 2) 3 times, CB, k 4, (CF, k 2) 3 times, CF **, k 4; rep from * 4 times, ending last rep at **, k 3, (k 1, p 1) 4 times.
Row 51: (K 1, p 1) 4 times, k 2,

* (CB, k 2) 3 times, CB, k 6, (CF, k 2) 3 times, CF, k 2; rep from * 4 times, (k 1, p 1) 4 times.

Row 53: (K 1, p 1) 4 times, k 1, * (CB, k 2) 3 times, CB, k 8, (CF, k 2) 3 times, CF; rep from * 4 times, k 1, (k 1, p 1) 4 times.

Row 55: (K 1, p 1) 4 times, k 1, change to D, k 2, change to MC, k 2, (CB, k 2) twice, CB, * k 10, (CF, k 2) 3 times **, right cross, k 2, (CB, k 2) twice, CB; rep from * 4 times, ending last rep at **, change to D, k 2, change to MC, k 1, (k 1, p 1) 4 times.

Row 57: (K 1, p 1) 4 times, k 1, CF, (CB, k 2) twice, CB, * k 12, (CF, k 2) twice, CF, CB **, CF, (CB, k 2) twice, CB; rep from * 4 times, ending last rep at **, k 1, (k 1, p 1) 4 times.

Row 59: (K 1, p 1) 4 times, k 2, left cross, (k 2, CB) twice, * k 14, (CF, k 2) twice **, (left cross, k 2) twice, CB, k 2, CB; rep from * 4 times, ending last rep at **, left cross, k 2, (k 1, p 1) 4 times.

Row 61: (K 1, p 1) 4 times, k 1, CB, CF, CB, k 2, CB, * k 16, CF, k 2 **, (CF, CB) 3 times, k 2, CB; rep from * 4 times, ending last rep at **, CF, CB, CF, k 1, (k 1, p 1) 4 times.

Row 63: (K 1, p 1) 4 times, k 1, change to C, k 2, change to MC, k 2, right cross, k 2, CB, * k 18, CF, k 2 **, (right cross, k 2) 3 times, CB; rep from * 4 times, ending last rep at **, right cross, k 2, change to C, k 2, change to MC, k 1, (k 1, p 1) 4 times.

Row 65: (K 1, p 1) 4 times, k 1, (CF, CB) twice, * k 20, (CF, CB) 4 times; rep from * 3 times, k 20, (CF, CB) twice, k 1, (k 1, p 1) 4 times.

Row 67: (K 1, p 1) 4 times, (k 2, left cross) twice, * k 22, (left cross, k 2) 3 times, left cross; rep from * 3 times, k 22, (left cross, k 2) twice, (k 1, p 1) 4 times.

Row 69: (K 1, p 1) 4 times, k 1, (CB, CF) twice, * k 20, (CB, CF) 4 times; rep from * 3 times, k 20, (CB, CF) twice, k 1, (k 1, p 1) 4 times.

Row 71: (K 1, p 1) 4 times, k 1, change to B, k 2, change to MC, k 2, right cross, k 2, CF, * k 18, CB, k 2 **, (right cross, k 2) 3 times, CF; rep from * 4 times, ending last rep at **, right cross, k 2, change to B, k 2, change to MC, k 1, (k 1, p 1) 4 times.

Row 73: (K 1, p 1) 4 times, k 1, CF, CB, CF, k 2, CF, * k 16, CB, k 2 **, (CB, CF) 3 times, k 2, CF; rep from * 4 times, ending last rep at **, CB, CF, CB, k 1, (k 1, p 1) 4 times.

Row 75: (K 1, p 1) 4 times, k 2, left cross, (k 2, CF) twice, * k 14, (CB, k 2) twice **, (left cross, k 2) twice, CF, k 2, CF; rep from * 4 times, ending last rep at **, left cross, k 2, (k 1, p 1) 4 times.

Row 77: (K 1, p 1) 4 times, k 1, CB, (CF, k 2) twice, CF, * k 12, (CB, k 2) twice, CB, CF **, CB, (CF, k 2) twice, CF; rep from * 4 times, ending last rep at **, k 1, (k 1, p 1) 4 times.

Row 79: (K 1, p 1) 4 times, k 1, change to A, k 2, change to MC, (k 2, CF) 3 times, * k 10, (CB, k 2) 3 times **, right cross, (k 2, CF) 3 times; rep from * 4 times, ending last rep at **, change to A, k 2, change to MC, k 1, (k 1, p 1) 4 times.

Rows 81–342: Rep rows 9–80, 3 times, then rep rows 9–54 once.

Rows 343–348: Work in seed st for 6 rows; BO after last row.

Afghan by Marjorie Hall
Loveland, Colorado

Stained Glass

Careful color selection gives this afghan the look of luminescence.
Slip stitch the "leading" in black to complete the look.

Materials 🧶 🧶 🧶

Worsted-weight acrylic yarn,
approximately:
31½ oz. (1,755 yd.) brown, A
10½ oz. (585 yd.) tan, B
7 oz. (390 yd.) cream, C
3½ oz. (215 yd.) off-white, D
14 oz. (780 yd.) black, E
3½ oz. (215 yd.) light rose, F
3½ oz. (215 yd.) rose, G
3½ oz. (215 yd.) dark rose, H
3½ oz. (215 yd.) mulberry, I
3½ oz. (215 yd.) raspberry, J
3½ oz. (215 yd.) lavender, K
3½ oz. (215 yd.) light purple, L
3½ oz. (215 yd.) purple, M
3½ oz. (215 yd.) blue, N
3½ oz. (215 yd.) light blue, O
3½ oz. (215 yd.) rust, P
3½ oz. (215 yd.) light rust, Q
3½ oz. (215 yd.) gold, R
3½ oz. (215 yd.) peach, S
3½ oz. (215 yd.) light peach, T
Worsted-weight brushed acrylic
    yarn, approximately:
7½ oz. (345 yd.) rose-and-green
    multicolored, U
5 oz. (230 yd.) purple-and-blue
    multicolored, V
2½ oz. (115 yd.) brown-and-
    gold multicolored, W
Size H afghan hook or size to
    obtain gauge
Size H crochet hook or size to
    obtain gauge
Yarn needle

Finished Size
Approximately 46" x 71"

Gauge
18 sts and 14 rows = 4"

Pattern Stitch

Purl: Holding yarn in front of work,
insert hook in vertical bar indicated,
yo and pull up lp.

Note: All sts worked in A, B, C, and
D are worked in foll pat:
Row 1: Work 1 row of afghan st.
Row 2: Step 1: Purl in first vertical
bar, (holding yarn in back of work,
pull up 2 lps in afghan st, purl in
next 2 sts) across. **Step 2:** Yo and
pull through 1 lp, (yo and pull
through 2 lps) across.
Row 3: Step 1: Pull up 1 lp in
afghan st, (purl in next 2 sts, pull up
2 lps in afghan st) across. **Step 2:**
Yo and pull through 1 lp, (yo and
pull through 2 lps) across.
  Rep rows 2 and 3 alternately.

Note: See page 148 for afghan st
directions. To change colors in
afghan st: **Step 1:** Drop yarn to ws of
work, insert hook under next vertical
bar and pull up lp with new color.
Do not carry yarn over more than
3 sts. **Step 2:** Yo and pull through
2 lps on hook until 1 lp of current
color rem on hook, drop yarn to ws
of work, pick up new color, yo and
pull through 2 lps on hook.

Left Panel
With afghan hook and A, ch 76.
Row 1: Work 1 row of afghan st:
76 sts.
Row 2: Step 1: Purl in first vertical
bar, (holding yarn in back of work,
pull up 2 lps in afghan st, purl in
next 2 sts) 6 times, pull up 1 lp in
afghan st, change to F, pull up 2 lps
in afghan st, change to A, pull up
1 lp in afghan st, (purl in next 2 sts,
pull up 2 lps in afghan st) 11 times,
purl in last 2 vertical bars: 76 lps on

hook. **Step 2:** Yo and pull through
1 lp, (yo and pull through 2 lps) 46
times, change to F, (yo and pull
through 2 lps) twice, change to A,
(yo and pull through 2 lps) 27 times.
Note: Read **Side Panel Chart** from
right to left.
Rows 3–247: Cont foll **Side Panel
Chart** on pages 104 and 105: 76 sts.
Row 248: Sl st in ea vertical bar
across; fasten off.

Right Panel
With afghan hook and A, ch 76.
Row 1: Work 1 row of afghan st:
76 sts.
Row 2: Step 1: Purl in first vertical
bar, (holding yarn in back of work,
pull up 2 lps in afghan st, purl in
next 2 sts) 11 times, pull up 1 lp in
afghan st, change to F, pull up 2 lps
in afghan st, change to A, pull up
1 lp in afghan st, (purl in next 2 sts,
pull up 2 lps in afghan st) 6 times,
purl in last 2 vertical bars: 76 lps on
hook. **Step 2:** Yo and pull through
1 lp, (yo and pull through 2 lps) 27
times, change to F, (yo and pull
through 2 lps) twice, change to A,
(yo and pull through 2 lps) 46 times.
Note: Read **Side Panel Chart** from
left to right.
Rows 3–247: Cont foll **Side Panel
Chart** on pages 104 and 105: 76 sts.
Row 248: Sl st in ea vertical bar
across; fasten off.

Center Panel
With afghan hook and A, ch 56.
Row 1: Work 1 row of afghan st:
56 sts.
Row 2: Step 1: Purl in first vertical
bar, (holding yarn in back of work,
pull up 2 lps in afghan st, purl in

(continued)

next 2 sts) 6 times, pull up 1 lp in afghan st, change to F, pull up 2 lps in afghan st, change to A, pull up 1 lp in afghan st, (purl in next 2 sts, pull up 2 lps in afghan st) 6 times, purl in last 2 vertical bars: 56 lps on hook. **Step 2:** Yo and pull through 1 lp, (yo and pull through 2 lps) 26 times, change to F, (yo and pull through 2 lps) twice, change to A, (yo and pull through 2 lps) 27 times. *Note:* Read **Center Panel Chart** from right to left.
Rows 3–124: Cont foll **Center Panel Chart** on page 103: 56 sts.
Note: Turn **Center Panel Chart** upside down for rows 125–247.
Rows 125–247: Reading **Center Panel Chart** upside down, rep rows 123–1 once: 56 sts.
Row 248: Sl st in ea vertical bar across; fasten off.

Assembly
With rs facing and using A, whip-stitch panels tog.
Outlines
With rs facing and crochet hook, join E in any diamond point with sl st, sl st across to next point. Rep to outline all diamonds and multicolored sections.

Border
Rnd 1 (rs): With rs facing and crochet hook, join E in top right corner with sl st, ch 1, 3 sc in same corner, sc in ea st across to next corner, * 3 sc in corner, sc in ea st across to next corner; rep from * around; join with sl st to beg sc.
Rnd 2: Ch 3, 3 dc in next sc, dc in ea sc across to next corner, * 3 dc in corner, dc in ea sc across to next corner; rep from * around; join with sl st to top of beg ch-3; fasten off.
Rnd 3 (ws): With ws facing and using crochet hook, join E in back of 3rd st of row 3 with sl st, ch 1, sc in same st and in ea st across to corner, * 3 sc in corner, sc in ea st across to next corner; rep from * around; join with sl st to beg sc.
Rnds 4 and 5: Ch 1, sc in back of next st of next row, sc in ea st across to corner, * 3 sc in corner; sc in ea st across to next corner; rep from * around; join with sl st to beg sc; fasten off.
Rnd 6 (rs): With rs facing, join E in top right corner with sl st, working in bk lps only of rnds 2 and 5, sl st in ea st around; join with sl st to beg sc; fasten off.

Afghan by Barbara Pawelko
Mt. Prospect, Illinois

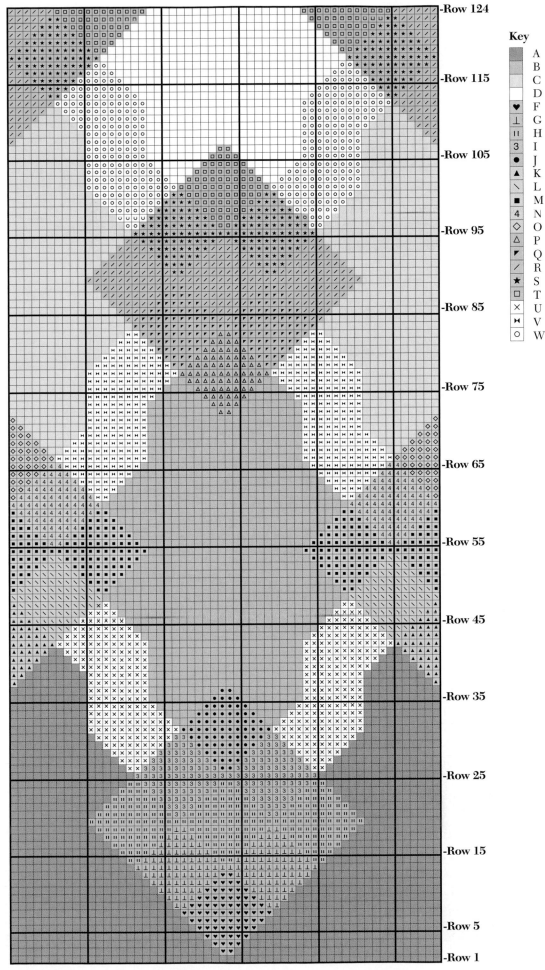

Center Panel Chart

Key

A
B
C
D
F
G
H
I
J
K
L
M
N
O
P
Q
R
S
T
U
V
W

-Row 124
-Row 115
-Row 105
-Row 95
-Row 85
-Row 75
-Row 65
-Row 55
-Row 45
-Row 35
-Row 25
-Row 15
-Row 5
-Row 1

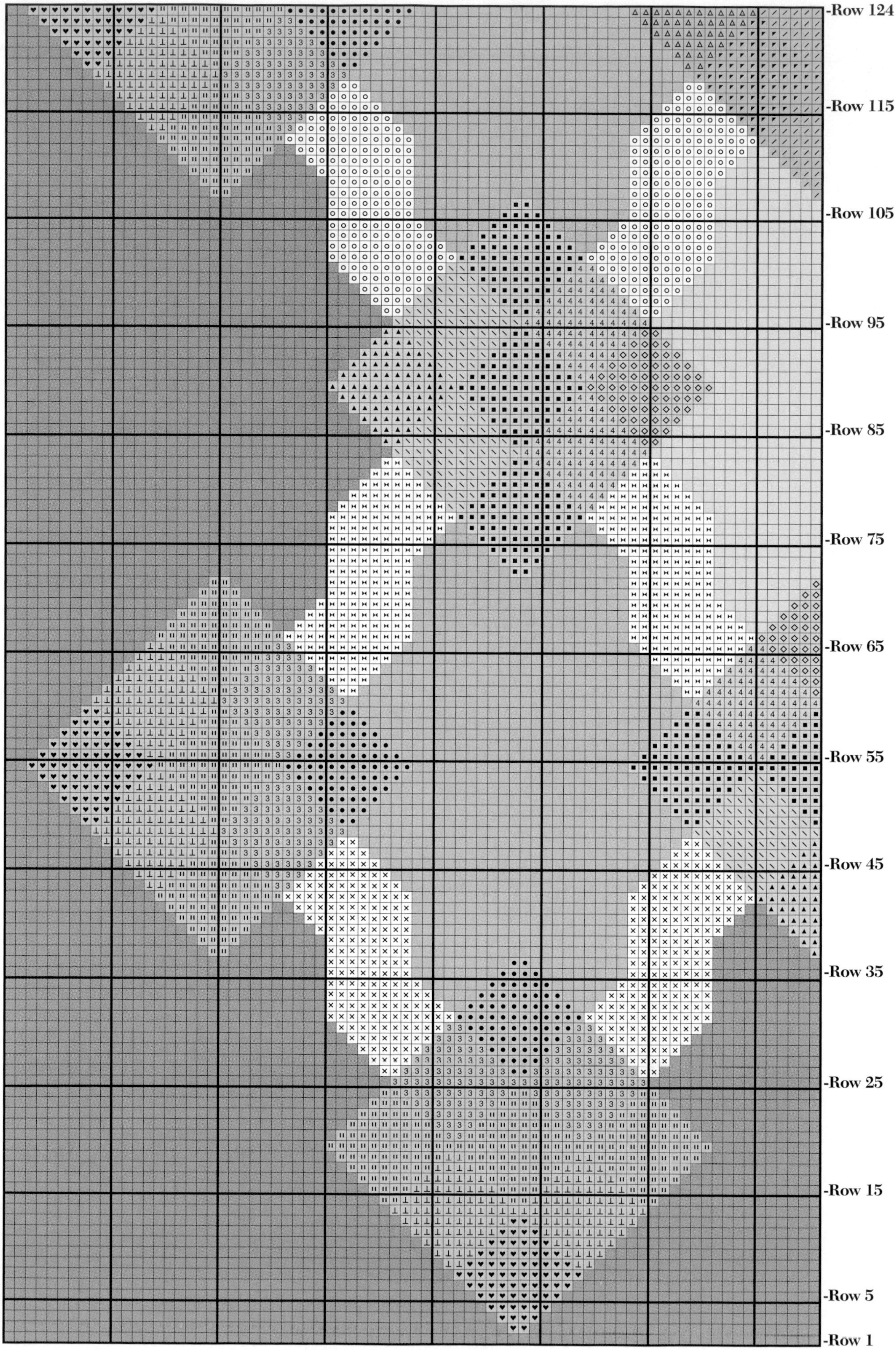

Bottom Side Panel Chart

-Row 124
-Row 115
-Row 105
-Row 95
-Row 85
-Row 75
-Row 65
-Row 55
-Row 45
-Row 35
-Row 25
-Row 15
-Row 5
-Row 1

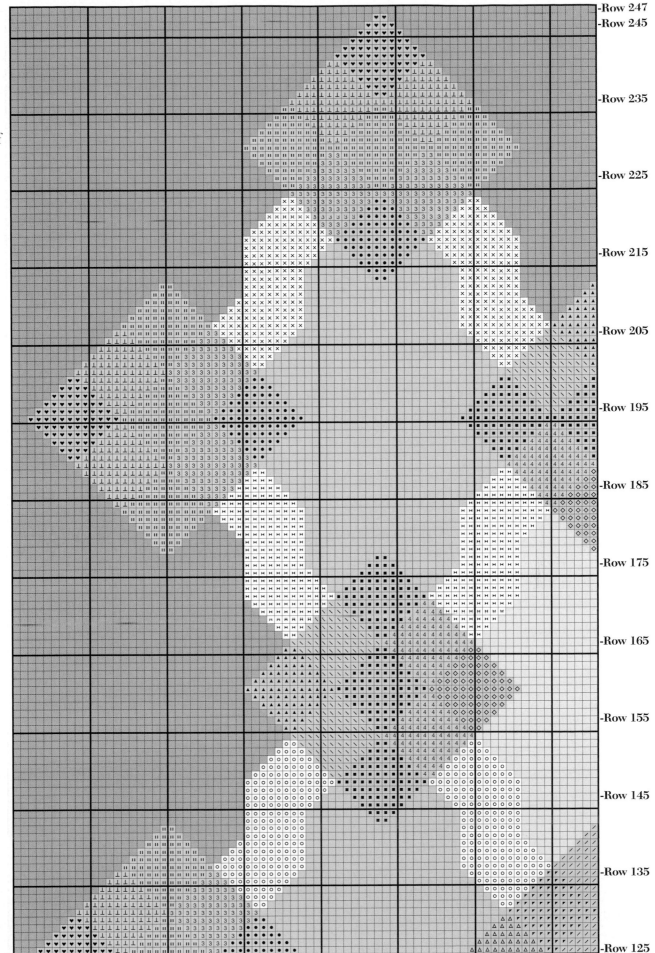

Note: Read *Chart* from right to left for Left Panel and from left to right for Right Panel. If necessary, make reverse photocopy of *Chart.*

-Row 247
-Row 245
-Row 235
-Row 225
-Row 215
-Row 205
-Row 195
-Row 185
-Row 175
-Row 165
-Row 155
-Row 145
-Row 135
-Row 125

Top Side Panel Chart

Heavenly Love

Combine two favorite motifs—angels and hearts worked in puffy picots—to express your deepest feelings for someone special.

Materials

Worsted-weight acrylic yarn,
approximately:
87½ oz. (5,325 yd.) cream
Size I afghan hook or size to
obtain gauge
Size I crochet hook or size to
obtain gauge
Yarn needle

Finished Size
Approximately 64" x 69"

Gauge
13 sts and 10 rows = 3"

Note: See page 148 for afghan st directions.

Heart Panel (Make 3.)
With afghan hook, ch 27.
Rows 1–5: Work 5 rows of afghan st: 27 sts.
Row 6: Step 1: Work same as **Step 1** of afghan st. **Step 2:** Referring to ***Heart Panel Chart*** on page 108, yo and pull through first lp on hook, (yo and pull through 2 lps on hook) 8 times, (ch 4, pull last ch through next lp on hook [picot made]) 3 times, (yo and pull through 2 lps on hook) 4 times, picot 3 times, (yo and pull through 2 lps on hook) 8 times.
Rows 7–94: Cont foll ***Heart Panel Chart*** as est.
Rows 95–208: Rep rows 51–94, twice, then rep rows 6–31 once.
Rows 209–213: Work 5 rows of afghan st: 27 sts.
Row 214: Sl st in ea vertical bar across; fasten off.
Edging
Rnd 1 (rs): With rs facing and using

crochet hook, join yarn in top right corner with sl st, ch 1, 2 sc in same st, sc in ea st across to next corner, * 3 sc in corner, sc evenly across to next corner; rep from * around; working in bk lp only, join with sl st in beg sc.
Rnd 2 (ws): Ch 1, turn; * working in ft lps only, (sk next sc, sc in next sc, sc in sk sc) across to last 2 sc, 2 sc in next 3 sc; rep from * around; join with sl st to beg sc.
Rnd 3: Ch 1, turn; working in bk lps only, sc in same sc and in ea sc across to corner, * 3 sc in corner, sc in ea sc across to next corner; rep from * around; join with sl st to beg sc.
Rnd 4: Rep rnd 2; fasten off.

Angel Panel (Make 2.)
With afghan hook, ch 61.
Rows 1–5: Work 5 rows of afghan st: 61 sts.

(continued)

Row 6: Step 1: Work same as **Step 1** of afghan st. **Step 2:** Referring to *Angel Panel Chart,* yo and pull through first lp on hook, (yo and pull through 2 lps on hook) 10 times, picot twice, (yo and pull through 2 lps on hook) twice, picot twice, ([yo and pull through 2 lps on hook] 13 times, picot twice), (yo and pull through 2 lps on hook) twice, picot twice, (yo and pull through 2 lps on hook) 10 times.

Rows 7–111: Cont foll *Angel Panel Chart* as est.

Rows 112–209: Rep rows 14–111 once.

Rows 210–213: Work 4 rows of afghan st: 61 sts.

Row 214: Sl st in ea vertical bar across; fasten off.

Edging

Work same as Heart Panel Edging.

Assembly

With rs facing, alternate panels beg and ending with Heart Panel and whipstitch tog.

Border

Rnd 1 (rs): With rs facing, working in bk lps only and using crochet hook, join yarn in top right corner with sl st, ch 1, 2 sc in same st, sc in ea sc across to next corner, * 3 sc in corner, sc evenly across to next corner; rep from * around; working in bk lp only, join with sl st in beg sc.

Rnds 2–4: Work same as rnds 2–4 for Heart Panel Edging.

Afghan by Alice Rayl
Niagara Falls, New York

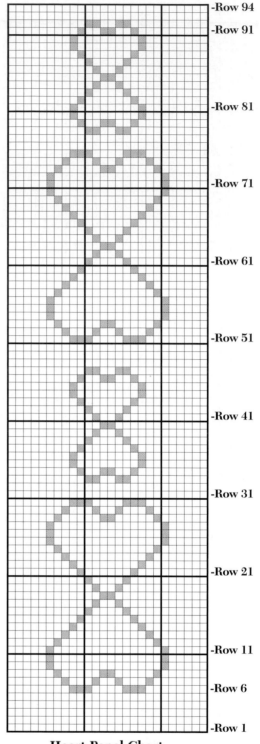

Heart Panel Chart

-Row 94
-Row 91
-Row 81
-Row 71
-Row 61
-Row 51
-Row 41
-Row 31
-Row 21
-Row 11
-Row 6
-Row 1

Key

☐ afghan
▨ picot

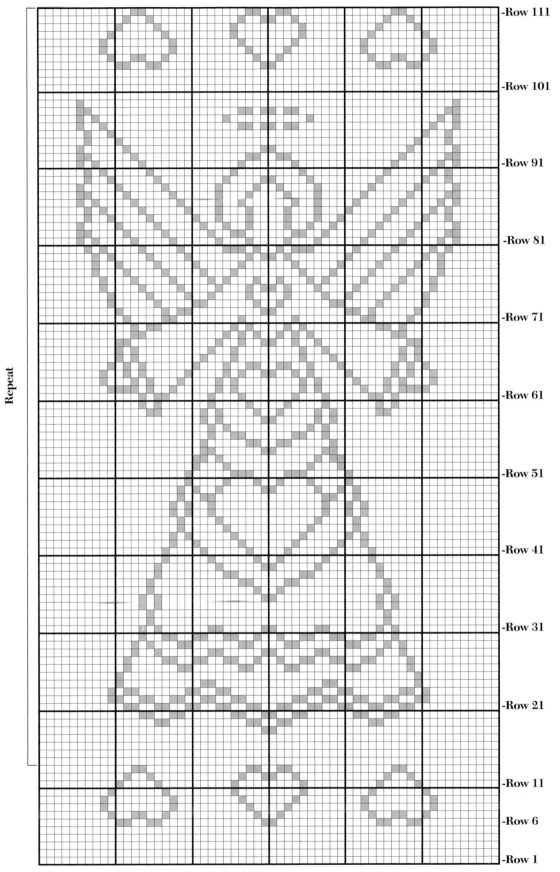

-Row 111

-Row 101

-Row 91

-Row 81

-Row 71

Repeat

-Row 61

-Row 51

-Row 41

-Row 31

-Row 21

-Row 11

-Row 6

-Row 1

Angel Panel Chart

Giraffes

This whimsical pattern captures the jungle look everyone is wild for, but it's sweet enough to be used in a nursery, too.

Materials

Worsted-weight acrylic yarn, approximately:
42 oz. (2,160 yd.) white
Size H crochet hook or size to obtain gauge

Finished Size

Approximately 39" x 50", without fringe

Gauge

15 sc and 14 rows = 4"

Pattern Stitches

Ldc: Dc in ft lp of next st 1 row below.

Bobble: 4 sc in ft lp only of st indicated, drop lp from hook, insert hook in first sc and pull dropped lp through.

Note: All rows are worked with rs facing. Leave 6" tail at beg and end of ea row for fringe.

Ch 193; fasten off.
Row 1 (rs): With rs facing, join yarn in first ch with sl st, ch 1, sc in same ch and in ea ch across; fasten off: 193 sc.

Rows 2–8: Join yarn in first sc with sl st, ch 1, sc in same sc and in next sc; working in bk lps only, sc in ea sc across to last 2 sc; working in both lps, sc in last 5 sc; fasten off: 193 sc.

Row 9: Referring to *Chart* on pages 112 and 113, join yarn in first sc with sl st, ch 1, sc in same sc and in next sc; working in bk lps only, sc in next 8 sc, (Ldc, sc in next sc) 6 times, sc in ea sc across to last 21 sc, (Ldc, sc in next sc) 6 times, sc in next 7 sc; working in both lps, sc in last 2 sc; fasten off: 193 sc.

Rows 10–142: Cont foll *Chart* as est.

Row 143: Join yarn in first sc with sl st, working in bk lps only, sl st in ea sc across; fasten off.

Fringe

For ea tassel, cut 1 (12") length of yarn. Knot yarn tog with 4 tails.

Afghan by Martha Gorka
Union City, Pennsylvania

Key

- □ sc in bk lp only
- • sc in both lps
- ◉ bobble
- ■ Ldc

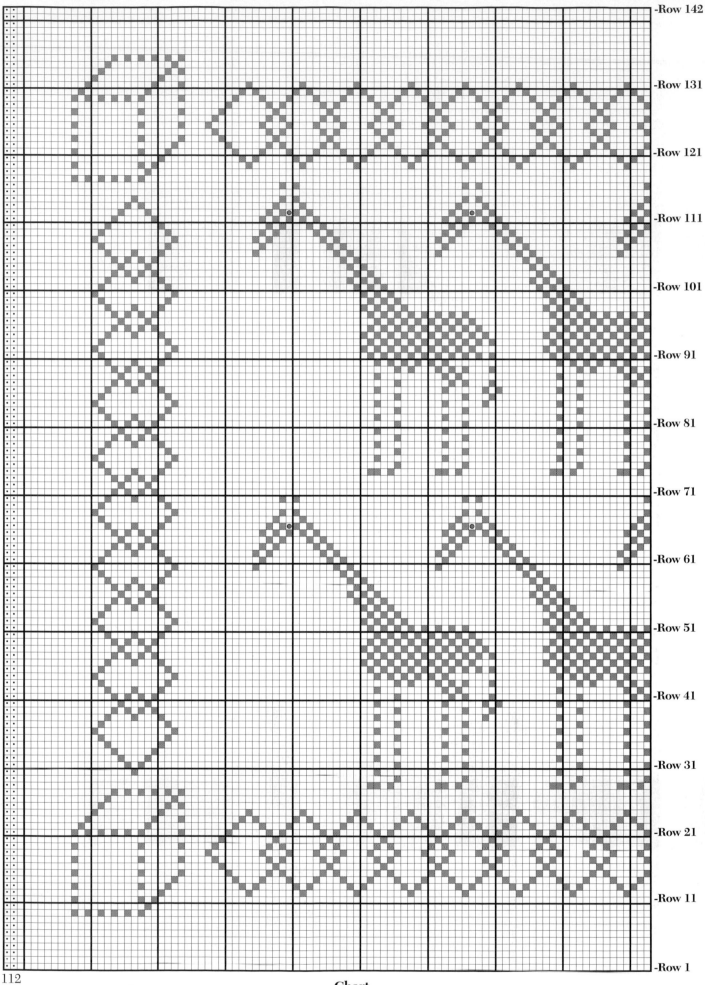

-Row 142

-Row 131

-Row 121

-Row 111

-Row 101

-Row 91

-Row 81

-Row 71

-Row 61

-Row 51

-Row 41

-Row 31

-Row 21

-Row 11

-Row 1

Chart

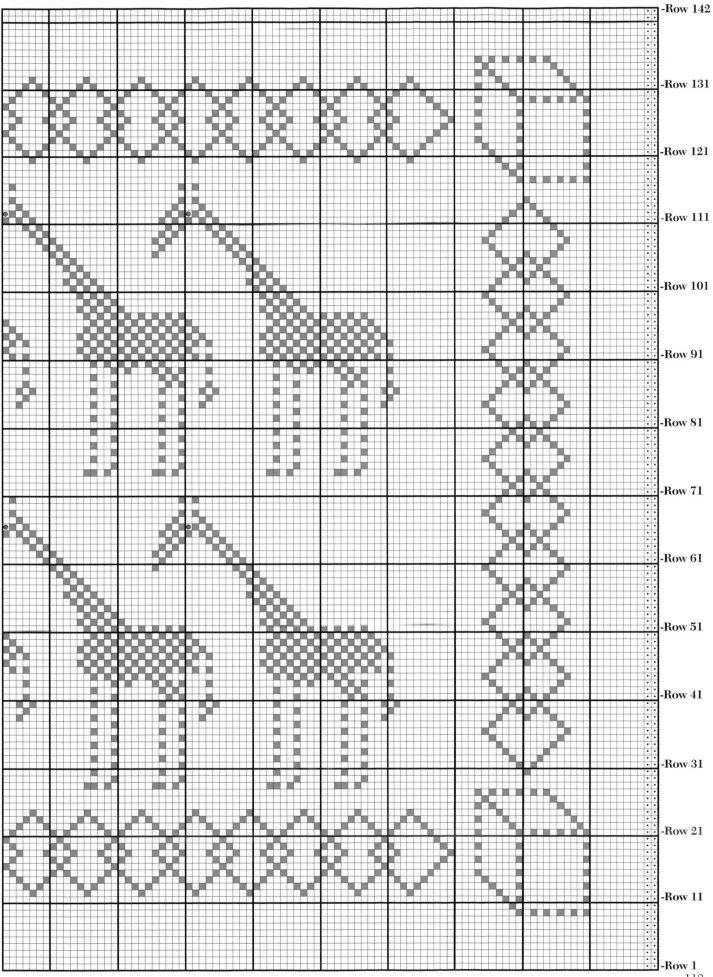

-Row 142

-Row 131

-Row 121

-Row 111

-Row 101

-Row 91

-Row 81

-Row 71

-Row 61

-Row 51

-Row 41

-Row 31

-Row 21

-Row 11

-Row 1

Chart

AFGHANS FOR LITTLE ONES

White Shells

This tiny wrap is perfect for the littlest angel. As she grows up, she can use the blanket for her favorite doll.

Materials

Sportweight acrylic yarn, approximately:
16 oz. (1,600 yd.) white
Size H crochet hook or size to obtain gauge

Finished Size
Approximately 27" x 33"

Gauge
In pat 4 shells and 11 rows = 5"

Pattern Stitch
Shell: 5 dc in st indicated.

Ch 119.
Row 1 (rs): 3 dc in 4th ch from hook, * sk next 2 chs, sc in next ch, sk 2 chs, shell in next ch; rep from * across to last ch, sc in last ch: 19 shells and 1 half-shell.
Rows 2–69: Ch 3 [counts as first dc throughout], turn; working in bk lp only, 3 dc in same st, * working in both lps, sc in top of next shell [3rd dc], working in bk lp only, shell in next sc; rep from * across; do not fasten off after last row: 19 shells and 1 half-shell.

Border
Note: Rnd 1 of Border is worked on 3 sides of afghan only.
Rnd 1 (rs): Ch 3, 4 dc in same st, (working in ends of rows, sc between next 2 shells, shell in next shell) across to next corner, (shell in next sc, sc in next shell) across to next corner, (working in ends of rows, sc between next 2 shells, shell in next shell) across to next corner, 3 dc in corner.
Rnd 2: Ch 1, sc in same st, ch 5, sl st in 3rd ch from hook [picot made], *sc in top of next shell, picot, sc in next sc, picot; rep from * around; join with sl st to beg sc; fasten off.

Afghan by Beatrice Taylor, Keyport, New Jersey

Tweed Stripes

Holding two strands of yarn together as you crochet makes a flecked fabric.

Materials

Sportweight acrylic yarn, approximately:
17½ oz. (1,960 yd.) white, MC
7 oz. (785 yd.) blue, A
5¼ oz. (590 yd.) green, B
Size K crochet hook or size to obtain gauge

Finished Size

Approximately 35" x 42", without fringe

Gauge

In pat, 12 sts and 12 rows = 4"

Note: Afghan is worked sideways holding 2 strands of yarn tog as 1 throughout. To change colors, work last yo of prev st with new color, dropping prev color to ws of work. Carry MC loosely across row.

With 1 strand ea MC and A, ch 125.
Row 1 (rs): Sc in 2nd ch from hook, dc in next ch, (sc in next ch, dc in next ch) across: 124 sts.

Rows 2–6: Ch 1, turn; sc in first dc, (dc in next sc, sc in next dc) across; drop A, pick up 1 strand MC after last row: 124 sts.
Rows 7 and 8: With 2 strands MC, rep row 2 twice; drop 1 strand MC, pick up 1 strand B after last row.
Rows 9–14: With 1 strand ea MC and B, rep row 2, 6 times; drop B, pick up 1 strand MC after last row.
Rows 15 and 16: With 2 strands MC, rep row 2 twice; drop 1 strand MC, pick up 1 strand A after last row.
Rows 17–22: With 1 strand ea MC and A, rep row 2, 6 times; drop A, pick up 1 strand MC after last row.
Rows 23–102: Rep rows 7–22, 5 times; do not fasten off.

Border

Rnd 1 (rs): With 2 strands MC, ch 1, turn; sc in first dc, (dc in next sc, sc in next dc) across to next corner, * (dc, sc, dc) in corner, sc in next st, (dc, sc) evenly across to next corner; rep from * around; join with sl st to beg sc.
Rnd 2: Ch 1, do not turn; working from left to right, sc in joining, * ch 1, sk next dc, sc in next sc; rep from * around; join with sl st to beg sc; fasten off.

Fringe

For ea tassel, referring to page 159 of General Directions, cut 5 (10") lengths ea of MC and contrasting color. Working across short ends and matching colors, knot 1 tassel in every ch-1 sp.

Afghan by Monica Kancel-Costello, Hannibal, Ohio

Pink and Blue

Not sure if the baby-to-be is a boy or a girl? Play it safe but stay traditional with stripes of both pink and blue.

Materials

Fingering-weight pompadour yarn, approximately:
7 oz. (740 yd.) white, MC
3½ oz. (370 yd.) pink, A
3½ oz. (370 yd.) blue, B
Size G crochet hook or size to obtain gauge
Yarn needle

Finished Size

Approximately 34" x 41", without fringe

Gauge

In pat, 6 V-sts and 9 rows = 4"

Pattern Stitches

V-st: (Dc, ch 1, dc) in st indicated.
Shell: 5 dc in st indicated.
Cl: (Yo, insert hook in next dc, yo and pull up lp, yo and pull through 2 lps) 5 times, yo and pull through all 6 lps on hook.

Note: Afghan is worked sideways. To change colors, work last yo of prev st with new color, dropping prev color to ws of work. Do not carry yarn across row.

With MC, ch 184.
Row 1 (rs): Dc in 4th ch from hook, ch 1, dc in same ch, (sk 2 chs, V-st in next st) across to last ch, dc in last ch: 60 V-sts.
Rows 2 and 3: Ch 3 [counts as dc throughout], turn; V-st in top of next V-st [ch-1 sp] and in ea V-st across; dc in top of beg ch-3.
Row 4: Ch 1, turn; sc in first dc, sc in ea dc and ea ch-1 sp across, change to A in last st: 182 sc.
Row 5: Ch 5 [counts as dc plus ch 2 throughout], turn; sk first 3 sc, shell in next sc, * sk next 4 sc, shell in next sc; rep from * across to last dc, dc in last dc, change to B: 36 shells.
Row 6: Ch 5, turn; (cl, ch 4) across, ch 2, dc in 3rd ch of beg ch-5; change to MC: 36 cls.
Row 7: Ch 1, turn; sc in first dc, 2 sc in ch-2 sp, * sc in next cl, 4 sc in next ch-4 sp; rep from * across to last cl, sc in last cl, 2 sc in ch-5 sp: 182 sc.
Row 8: Ch 3, turn; sk first sc, V-st in next sc, * sk 2 sc, V-st in next sc; rep from * across to last 3 sc, sk 2 sc, dc in last sc: 60 V-sts.
Rows 9–11: Rep rows 2–4, change to B in last st of last row.
Row 12: Rep row 5, change to A in last st.

Rows 13–15: Rep rows 6–8.
Rows 16–73: Rep rows 2–15, 4 times, then rep row 2 twice; fasten off after last row.

Border

Rnd 1 (rs): With rs facing, join MC in top right corner with sl st, ch 1, sc in same st, sc in ea dc and ea ch-1 sp across to corner, * 3 sc in corner, sc evenly across to next corner; rep from * around, 2 sc in corner; join with sl st to beg sc.
Rnd 2: Ch 1, sc in same st and in ea sc across to corner, * 3 sc in corner, sc evenly across to next corner; rep from * around, 2 sc in corner; join with sl st to beg sc; fasten off.

Fringe

For ea tassel, referring to page 159 of General Directions, cut 5 (11") lengths MC. Working across short ends, knot 1 tassel in every 3rd st.

Afghan by Connie E. Clark, Wintersville, Ohio

Color Block

With color changes every two stitches, each pastel block
is a checkerboard of color and white.

Materials

Fingering-weight acrylic yarn,
approximately:
16 oz. (1,600 yd.) white, MC
4 oz. (400 yd.) pink, A
4 oz. (400 yd.) blue, B
4 oz. (400 yd.) yellow, C
4 oz. (400 yd.) green, D
4 oz. (400 yd.) lavender, E
Size G crochet hook or size to
obtain gauge

Finished Size

Approximately 34" x 45", without
fringe

Gauge

20 sts and 11 rows = 4"

Note: To change colors, work last yo
of prev st with new color, dropping
prev color to ws of work. Do not
carry yarn across more than 3 sts.

Directions

With MC, ch 170.
Row 1 (ws): Dc in 4th ch from
hook, (change to A, dc in next 2 chs,
change to MC, dc in next 2 chs) 6
times, (change to B, dc in next 2 chs,
change to MC, dc in next 2 chs) 6
times, (change to C, dc in next 2 chs,
change to MC, dc in next 2 chs) 6
times, (change to D, dc in next
2 chs, change to MC, dc in next
2 chs) 6 times, (change to C, dc in
next 2 chs, change to MC, dc in next
2 chs) 6 times, (change to B, dc in
next 2 chs, change to MC, dc in next
2 chs) 6 times, (change to A, dc in
next 2 chs, change to MC, dc in next
2 chs) 5 times, change to A, dc in
last 2 chs, change to MC: 168 dc.
Rows 2–14: Ch 3, turn; dc in next
dc, (change to A, dc in next 2 dc,
change to MC, dc in next 2 dc) 6
times, (change to B, dc in next 2 dc,
change to MC, dc in next 2 dc) 6
times, (change to C, dc in next 2 dc,
change to MC, dc in next 2 dc) 6
times, (change to D, dc in next 2 dc,
change to MC, dc in next 2 dc) 6
times, (change to C, dc in next 2 dc,
change to MC, dc in next 2 dc) 6
times, (change to B, dc in next 2 dc,
change to MC, dc in next 2 dc) 6
times, (change to A, dc in next 2 dc,
change to MC, dc in next 2 dc) 5
times, change to A, dc in last 2 dc,
change to MC: 168 dc.
Rows 15–28: Rep row 2, 14 times,
working in foll color sequence: B, C,
D, E, D, C, B.
Rows 29–42: Rep row 2, 14 times,
working in foll color sequence: C, D,
E, A, E, D, C.
Rows 43–56: Rep row 2, 14 times,
working in foll color sequence: D, E,
A, B, A, E, D.
Rows 57–70: Rep row 2, 14 times,
working in foll color sequence: E, A,
B, C, B, A, E.
Rows 71–84: Rep rows 43–56.
Rows 85–98: Rep rows 29–42.
Rows 99–112: Rep rows 15–28.
Rows 113–126: Rep row 2, 14
times; fasten off after last row.

Fringe

For ea tassel, referring to page 159
of General Directions, cut 2 (14")
lengths ea of MC and contrasting
color. Working across short ends,
knot 1 tassel between every 2 MC dc
in foll color sequence: * A, B **, C,
D, E; rep from * across, ending last
rep at **.

*Afghan by Jewel Ferguson,
Coweta, Oklahoma*

Tic-tac-toe

Bedtime will seem like game time with this fun afghan. If you like, cut some markers from felt and play a round in the center square.

(continued)

Materials

Worsted-weight acrylic yarn, approximately:
21 oz. (1,280 yd.) white, MC
3½ oz. (215 yd.) purple, A
7 oz. (430 yd.) black, B
7 oz. (430 yd.) red, C
3½ oz. (215 yd.) yellow, D
3½ oz. (215 yd.) fuchsia, E
3½ oz. (215 yd.) dark teal, F
3½ oz. (215 yd.) light teal, G
3½ oz. (215 yd.) blue, H
3½ oz. (215 yd.) lavender, I
Size H afghan hook or size to obtain gauge
Size H crochet hook or size to obtain gauge

Finished Size
Approximately 45" x 52"

Gauge
19 sts and 14 rows = 4"

Note: See page 148 for afghan st directions. To change colors in afghan st: **Step 1:** Drop yarn to ws of work, insert hook under next vertical bar and pull up lp with new color. Do not carry yarn over more than 3 sts. **Step 2:** Yo and pull through 2 lps on hook until 1 lp of current color rem on hook, drop yarn to ws of work, pick up new color, yo and pull through 2 lps on hook.

Side Panel (Make 2.)
With afghan hook and MC, ch 68.
Rows 1–3: Work 3 rows of afghan st: 68 sts.
Rows 4–177: Foll *Side Panel Chart* on page 124: 68 sts.
Row 178: Sl st in ea vertical bar across; fasten off.
Edging
Row 1 (rs): With crochet hook and rs facing, join C in bottom right corner with sl st, ch 1, sc in same st and in ea st across to next corner; fasten off.

Center Panel
With afghan hook and MC, ch 68.
Rows 1–3: Work 3 rows of afghan st: 68 sts.
Rows 4–60: Foll *Center Panel Chart A* on page 125: 68 sts.
Rows 61–120: Rep rows 1–60 once, omitting Xs and Os: 68 sts.
Rows 121–177: Foll *Center Panel Chart B* on page 125: 68 sts.
Row 178: Sl st in ea vertical bar across; fasten off.
Edging
Row 1 (rs): Work same as Side Panel edging.
Row 2 (rs): With rs facing and using crochet hook, join C in top left corner with sl st, ch 1, sc in same st and in ea st across to next corner; fasten off.

Assembly
Join Left Side Panel to Center Panel as folls: With ws tog and using crochet hook, join C in corner with sl st, working in ft lps only, sl st in ea sc across; fasten off. Turn Right Side Panel upside down and sl st to Center Panel as est.

Border
Rnd 1 (rs): With rs facing and using crochet hook, join C in any corner with sl st, ch 1, 2 sc in same st, sc evenly across to next corner, * 3 sc in corner, sc evenly across to

next corner; rep from * around; join with sl st to beg sc.

Rnds 2 and 3: Ch 1, working in bk lps only, * 3 sc in corner, sc in ea sc across to next corner; rep from * around; join with sl st to beg sc; fasten off.

Afghan by Barbara Pawelko, Mt. Prospect, Illinois

Key

MC

A

B

C

D

E

F

G

H

I

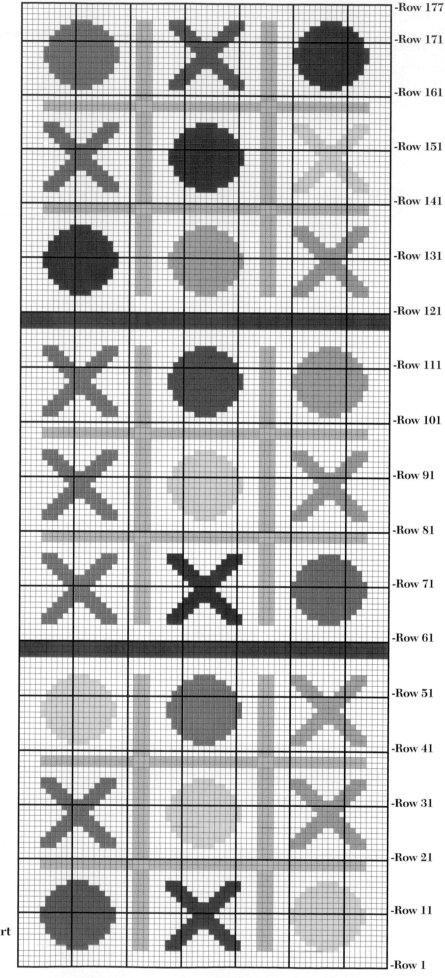

Side Panel Chart

124

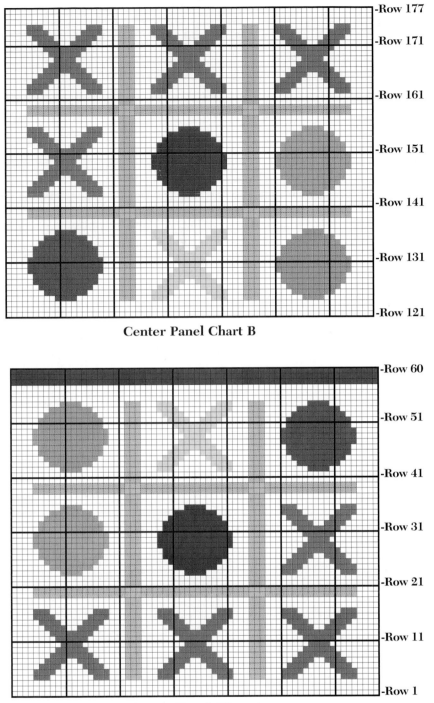

-Row 177
-Row 171
-Row 161
-Row 151
-Row 141
-Row 131
-Row 121

Center Panel Chart B

-Row 60
-Row 51
-Row 41
-Row 31
-Row 21
-Row 11
-Row 1

Center Panel Chart A

Spots and Stripes

Increase your knitting knowledge with textured stitches. Each block is knitted from corner to corner, forming two triangles.

Materials

Sportweight acrylic yarn, approximately:
17½ oz. (1,850 yd.) white, MC
12¼ oz. (1,295 yd.) aqua, CC
Size 4 knitting needles or size to obtain gauge
Size E crochet hook or size to obtain gauge
Yarn needle

Finished Size

Approximately 36" x 45"

Gauge

26 sts = 4"
Ea block = 4½"

Pattern Stitches

Inc: K in front and back of next st.
P-inc: P in front and back of next st.
Inc 2 sts: K in front and back of next st, then k in front of same st again.
K2tog [dec]: Insert right needle in front of next 2 sts from left to right, complete k st.
K2tog in back [dec]: Insert right needle in back of next 2 sts from right to left, complete k st.
P2tog [dec]: Insert right needle in front of next 2 sts from right to left, complete p st.
P3tog [dec]: Insert right needle in front of next 3 sts from right to left, complete p st.

Triangle-Square (Make 80.)

With MC, CO 3 sts.
Row 1 (rs): P across: 3 sts.
Row 2: Inc twice, k 1: 5 sts.
Row 3: P across: 5 sts.
Row 4: Inc, k across to last 2 sts, inc, k 1: 7 sts.
Row 5: P 3, inc 2 sts, p 3: 9 sts.
Row 6: Inc, k 2, p-inc twice, p 1, k 1, inc, k 1: 13 sts.
Row 7: P 4, k 5, p 4: 13 sts.
Row 8: Inc, k 3, p 5, k 2, inc, k 1: 15 sts.
Row 9: P 5, k2tog in back, k 1, k2tog, p 5: 13 sts.
Row 10: Inc, k 4, p 3, k 3, inc, k 1: 15 sts.
Row 11: P 6, sl next st, k2tog, psso, p 6: 13 sts.
Row 12: Inc, K across to last 2 sts, inc, k 1: 15 sts.
Row 13: P 3, inc 2 sts, p 7, inc 2 sts, p 3: 19 sts.
Row 14: Inc, k 2, * p-inc twice, p 1 **, k 7; rep from * to ** once, k 1, inc, k 1: 25 sts.
Row 15: P 4, k 5, p 7, k 5, p 4: 25 sts.
Row 16: Inc, k 3, (p 5, k 7) twice, p 5, k 2, inc, k 1: 27 sts.
Row 17: P 5, * k2tog in back, k 1, k2tog **, p 7; rep from * to ** once, p 5: 23 sts.
Row 18: Inc, k 4, p 3, k 7, p 3, k 3, inc, k 1: 25 sts.
Row 19: P 6, * sl next st, k2tog, psso **, p 7; rep from * to ** once, inc 2 sts, k 1: 21 sts.
Row 20: Inc, k across to last 2 sts, inc, k 1: 23 sts.
Row 21: P 3, (inc 2 sts, p 7) twice, inc 2 sts, p 3: 29 sts.
Row 22: Inc, k 2, (p-inc twice, p 1, k 7) twice, p-inc twice, p 1, k 1, inc, k 1: 37 sts.

(continued)

Row 23: P 4, (k 5, p 7) twice, k 5, p 4: 37 sts.
Row 24: Inc, k 3, (p 5, k 7) twice, p 5, k 2, inc, k 1: 39 sts.
Row 25: P 5, (k2tog in back, k 1, k2tog, p 7) twice, k2tog in back, k 1, k2tog, p 5: 33 sts.
Row 26: Inc, k 4, (p 3, k 7) twice, p 3, k 3, inc, k 1: 35 sts.
Row 27: P 6, (sl next st, k2tog, psso, p 7) twice, sl next st, k2 tog, psso, p 6: 29 sts.
Row 28: Inc, k across to last 2 sts, inc, k 1: 31 sts.
Row 29: P 3 (inc 2 sts, p 7) 3 times, inc 2 sts, p 3: 39 sts.
Row 30: Inc, k 2, (p-inc twice, p 1, k 7) 3 times, p-inc twice, p 1, k 1, inc, k 1: 49 sts.
Row 31: P 4, (k 5, p 7) 3 times, k 5, p 4: 49 sts.
Row 32: Inc, k 3, (p 5, k 7) 3 times, p 5, k 2, inc, k 1: 51 sts.

Row 33: P 5, (k2tog in back, k 1, k2tog, p 7) 3 times, k2tog in back, k 1, k2tog, p 5: 43 sts.
Row 34: Inc, k 4, (p 3, k 7) 3 times, p 3, k 3, inc, k 1: 45 sts.
Row 35: P 6, (sl next st, k2tog, psso, p 7) 3 times, sl next st, k2tog, psso, p 6: 37 sts.
Row 36: Inc, k across to last 2 sts, inc, k 1: 39 sts.
Row 37: Join CC, k2tog in back, k across: 38 sts.
Row 38: P2tog, p across: 37 sts.
Rows 39 and 40: K2tog in back, k across: 35 sts after last row.
Rows 41–72: Rep rows 38–40, 10 times, then rep rows 38 and 39 once.
Row 73: P3tog: 1 st; BO.

Assembly
Afghan is 10 blocks long and 8 blocks wide. With rs tog and referring to photo for placement, whipstitch blocks tog.

Border
Rnd 1 (rs): With rs facing and using crochet hook, join CC in top right corner with sl st, ch 1, 2 sc in same st, sc evenly across to next corner, * 3 sc in corner, sc evenly across to next corner; rep from * around; join with sl st to beg sc; fasten off.
Rnd 2: With rs facing, join MC in top right corner with sl st, ch 1, sc in same st, (ch 3, sl st in 3rd ch from hook [picot made], sc in next sc) twice, * (picot, sk next sc, sc in next sc) across to next corner (picot, sc in next sc) 3 times; rep from * around, picot; join with sl st to beg sc; fasten off.

Afghan by Marguerite Wilson
New Brighton, Minnesota

Filet Hearts

Follow a simple filet crochet chart for rows of sweet hearts
in gentle pastels. Complete the throw with a wide
multicolored border and lacy picots.

Materials

Sportweight acrylic yarn, approximately:
- 4 oz. (400 yd.) white, MC
- 2 oz. (200 yd.) pastel green, A
- 2 oz. (200 yd.) pink, B
- 2 oz. (200 yd.) lavender, C
- 2 oz. (200 yd.) yellow, D
- 2 oz. (200 yd.) pastel blue, E
- Size D crochet hook or size to obtain gauge

Finished Size

Approximately 37" x 37"

Gauge

26 dc and 13 rows = 4"

Pattern Stitches

Block over Space: Dc in ch-1 sp, dc in next dc.

Space over Space: Ch 1, sk ch-1 sp, dc in next dc.

Space over Block: Ch 1, sk next dc, dc in next dc.

Note: To change colors, work last yo of prev st with new color, dropping prev color to ws of work. Do not carry yarn across row.

Directions

With A, ch 185.

Row 1: Dc in 4th ch from hook and in ea ch across: 182 dc.

Rows 2–5: Ch 3 [counts as first dc throughout], turn; referring to *Chart,* dc in next 36 dc, (work Space over Space 19 times, dc in next 34 dc) twice, dc in last dc: 38 ch-1 sps.

Rows 6–19: Cont foll *Chart* as est; change to B in last st of last row.

Rows 20–37: Cont foll *Chart* as est; change to C in last st of last row.

Rows 38–90: Rep rows 2–37, once, then rep rows 2–18 once, foll color sequence: 18 rows ea C and D, 17 rows E; do not fasten off.

Row 91: Ch 3, turn; dc in next dc and in ea dc and ch-1 sp across: 182 dc; fasten off.

Border

Rnd 1 (rs): With rs facing, join MC in top right corner with sl st, ch 3,

2 dc in same dc, dc in ea dc across to corner, * 3 dc in corner, work 181 dc evenly sp across to next corner; rep from * around; join with sl st to top of beg ch-3; fasten off.

Rnd 2: With rs facing, join A in top right corner with sl st, ch 4 [counts as dc plus ch 1 throughout], (dc, ch 1, dc) in same corner, (ch 1, sk next dc, dc in next dc) across to next corner, * ([dc, ch 1] twice, dc) in next corner, (ch 1, sk next dc, dc in next dc) across to next corner; rep from * around; join with sl st to beg dc; fasten off.

Rnd 3: With rs facing, join MC in top right corner with sl st, ch 3, 2 dc in same dc, dc in ea dc and ea ch across to corner, * 3 dc in corner, dc in ea dc and ea ch across to next corner; rep from * around; join with sl st to top of beg ch-3; fasten off.

Rnds 4–11: Rep rnds 2 and 3 alternately, 4 times, foll color sequence: 1 rnd ea B, MC, C, MC, D, MC, E, MC; do not fasten off after last row.

Rnd 12: Ch 3, dc in same corner, (ch 3, sl st in 3rd ch from hook [picot made], dc in same corner, * (ch 1, sk next dc, dc in next dc, picot, sk next dc, dc in next dc) across to next corner, (ch 1, dc, picot, 2 dc) in corner, (picot, sk next dc, dc in next dc, ch 1, sk next dc, dc in next dc) across to next corner **, (picot, 2 dc, picot, dc) in corner; rep from * to ** once, picot; join with sl st to top of beg ch-3.

Rnd 13: Sl st in next dc, ch 6, picot, ch 3, sk next dc, dc in next dc, * ch 3, picot, ch 3, sk next dc **, dc in next dc; rep from * around, ending last rep at **; join with sl st to 3rd ch of beg ch-6; fasten off.

Afghan by Laurie Halama, Independence, Wisconsin

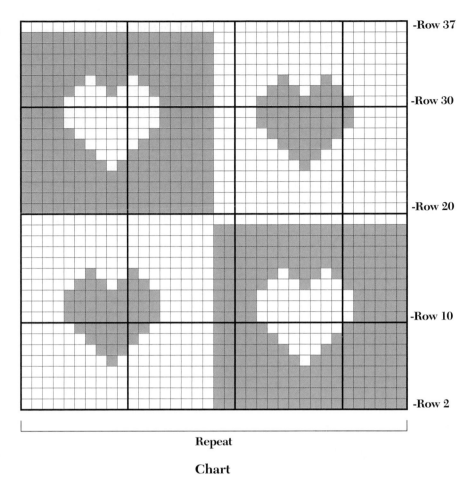

-Row 37
-Row 30
-Row 20
-Row 10
-Row 2

Repeat

Chart

Key

▓	2 dc
☐	ch 1, sk 1 st or sp, dc

Sherbet Stripes

Capture the cool colors of raspberry and lime sherbet in a soft and inviting throw.

Materials
Chunky-weight brushed acrylic yarn, approximately:
21 oz. (945 yd.) white, MC
12 oz. (540 yd.) pink, A
15 oz. (675 yd.) mint, B
Size J crochet hook or size to obtain gauge

Finished Size
Approximately 33" x 45", without fringe

Gauge
In pat, 2 shells and 6 rows = 3"

Pattern Stitches
Shell: (2 dc, ch 1, 2 dc) in st indicated.
FPdc: Yo, insert hook from front to back around st indicated, yo and pull up lp, (yo and pull through 2 lps) twice.

Note: Afghan is worked sideways. To change colors, work last yo of prev st with new color, dropping prev color to ws of work. Do not carry yarn across row.

With MC, ch 123.
Row 1 (ws): Shell in 5th ch from hook, * sk next ch, dc in next ch, sk next ch, shell in next ch; rep from * across to last 2 chs, sk next ch, dc in last ch: 30 shells.
Row 2 (rs): Ch 3 [counts as dc throughout], turn; (shell in top of next shell [ch-1 sp], sk 2 dc, FPdc around next dc) across to last shell, shell in top of last shell, dc in top of beg ch-3, change to A.
Rows 3 and 4: Ch 3, turn; (shell in top of next shell, FPdc around next FPdc) across to last shell, shell in top of last shell, dc in top of beg ch-3; change to MC after last row.
Rows 5–64: Rep row 3, 60 times, foll color sequence: * 2 rows ea MC, B **, MC, A; rep from * 6 times, then rep from * to ** once; fasten off after last row.

Edging
Row 1 (ws): With ws facing, join B in bottom left corner with sl st, ch 3, (shell in next shell [bet 2-dc grps], FPdc around next dc) across to last shell, shell in last shell, dc in corner ch.
Row 2: Ch 3, turn; (shell in top of next shell, FPdc around next FPdc) across to last shell, shell in top of last shell, dc in top of beg ch-3; fasten off.

Fringe
For ea tassel, referring to page 159 of General Directions, cut 8 (11") lengths of yarn. Working across short ends and matching colors, knot 1 tassel in every stripe.

Afghan by Monica Kancel-Costello, Hannibal, Ohio

Puffed Shells

This quick-to-stitch afghan looks great in multicolored yarn. The triple crochet shells puff gently for added softness.

Materials

Worsted-weight acrylic yarn, approximately:
27 oz. (1,605 yd.) pastel multicolored
Size I crochet hook or size to obtain gauge

Finished Size

Approximately 38" x 38", without fringe

Gauge

In pat, 2 shells and 8 rows = 5"

Pattern Stitches

Shell: 7 tr in st indicated.
V-st: (dc, ch 2, dc) in st indicated.

Note: Afghan is worked sideways.

Ch 92.
Row 1 (rs): Sc in 2nd ch from hook, * ch 2, sk next 2 chs, V-st in next ch, ch 2, sk next 2 chs, sc in next ch; rep from * across: 15 V-sts.
Row 2: Ch 4 [counts as tr throughout], turn; 3 tr in same sc, * ch 1, sc in top of next V-st [ch-2 sp], ch 1 **, shell in next sc; rep from * across, ending last rep at **, 4 tr in last sc: 14 shells and 2 half-shells.
Row 3: Ch 1, turn; sc in first tr, * ch 2, V-st in next sc, ch 2, sk next 3 tr, sc in 4th tr [top of shell]; rep from * across: 15 V-sts.
Rows 4–60: Rep rows 2 and 3 alternately, 28 times, then rep row 2 once; do not fasten off after last row.

Border

Note: Border is worked on 3 sides of afghan only.
Rnd 1 (ws): Sc in same st, (sc evenly across to next corner, 3 sc in corner) twice, sc evenly across to next corner, sc in next corner.
Rnd 2 (rs): Ch 1, turn; sc in same sc, (sc in ea sc across to next corner, 3 sc in corner) twice, sc in ea sc across to next corner, sc in next corner; fasten off.

Fringe

For ea tassel, referring to page 159 of General Directions, cut 2 (7") lengths yarn. Working across short ends, knot 1 tassel in ea st.

Afghan by Pamela DeSantis, Palmyra, Pennsylvania

Rainbow Ripple

Combine pastel panels of chevrons for a bold ripple design.
The afghan-stitch variation makes for a thick blanket.

Materials 🧶🧶

Worsted-weight acrylic yarn,
  approximately:
24 oz. (1,360 yd.) white, MC
8 oz. (455 yd.) coral, A
8 oz. (455 yd.) pink, B
8 oz. (455 yd.) lavender, C
8 oz. (455 yd.) light blue, D
8 oz. (455 yd.) light green, E
8 oz. (455 yd.) yellow, F
Size H crochet hook or size to
  obtain gauge
Size J afghan hook or size to
  obtain gauge

Finished Size

Approximately 50" x 65"

Gauge

20 sts and 17 rows = 4½"

Note: See page 148 for afghan st
directions. To change colors, drop
yarn to ws of work, yo with new color
and pull through 2 lps on hook.

Panel (Make 9.)

With crochet hook and B, ch 20.
Row 1: Step 1: With afghan hook,
work step 1 of afghan st. **Step 2:**
Yo and pull through 1 lp on hook,
(yo and pull through 2 lps on hook) 9
times, ch 1, (yo and pull through
2 lps on hook) 10 times.
Row 2: Step 1: Sk first st, (insert
hook in sp between next 2 vertical
bars, yo and pull up lp) 8 times,
(insert hook in next ch, yo and pull
up lp) twice, (insert hook in sp
between next 2 vertical bars, yo and
pull up lp) 8 times, sk last sp, insert
hook under last vertical bar, yo and
pull up lp. **Step 2:** Yo and pull
through 1 lp on hook, (yo and pull

through 2 lps on hook) 9 times, ch 1,
(yo and pull through 2 lps on hook)
10 times.
Rows 3–9: Rep row 2, 7 times.
Row 10: Step 1: Work same as step
1 of row 2. **Step 2:** Yo and pull
through 1 lp on hook, (yo and pull
through 2 lps on hook) 4 times,
change to MC, (yo and pull through
2 lps on hook) 4 times, ch 1, (yo and
pull through 2 lps on hook) 10 times.
Row 11: Step 1: Work same as step
1 of row 2. **Step 2:** Yo and pull
through 1 lp on hook, (yo and pull
through 2 lps on hook) 4 times,
change to C, (yo and pull through
2 lps on hook) 4 times, ch 1, (yo and
pull through 2 lps on hook) 10 times.
Rows 12–22: Rep row 2, 9 times,
then rep rows 10 and 11 once,
changing to D in last row.
Rows 23–33: Rep row 2, 9 times,
then rep rows 10 and 11 once,
changing to E in last row.
Rows 34–44: Rep row 2, 9 times,
then rep rows 10 and 11 once,
changing to F in last row.
Rows 45–55: Rep row 2, 9 times,
then rep rows 10 and 11 once,
changing to A in last row.
Rows 56–65: Rep row 2, 9 times,
then rep row 10 once.
Rows 66–70: Rep row 2, 4 times,
then rep row 11 once, changing to B
in last row.
Rows 71–76: Rep row 2, 4 times,
then rep rows 10 and 11 once,
changing to C in last row.
Rows 77–82: Rep row 2, 4 times,
then rep rows 10 and 11 once,
changing to D in last row.
Rows 83–88: Rep row 2, 4 times,
then rep rows 10 and 11 once,
changing to E in last row.
Rows 89–94: Rep row 2, 4 times,
then rep rows 10 and 11 once,

changing to F in last row.
Rows 95–100: Rep row 2, 4 times,
then rep rows 10 and 11 once,
changing to A in last row.
Rows 101–105: Rep row 2, 4 times,
then rep row 10 once.
Rows 106–110: Rep row 2, 4 times,
then rep row 11 once, changing to A
in last row.
Rows 111–116: Rep rows 89–94.
Rows 117–122: Rep rows 83–88.
Rows 123–128: Rep rows 77–82.
Rows 129–134: Rep rows 71–76.
Rows 135–140: Rep row 2, 4 times,
then rep rows 10 and 11 once,
changing to B in last row.
Rows 141–150: Rep rows 101–110
once.
Rows 151–161: Rep rows 34–44
once.
Rows 162–172: Rep rows 23–33
once.
Rows 173–183: Rep rows 12–22
once.
Rows 184–194: Rep row 2, 9 times,
then rep rows 10 and 11 once,
changing to B in last row.
Rows 195–203: Rep row 2, 9 times.
Row 204: Using crochet hook, ch 1,
sc in first sp between vertical bars
and in next 8 sps, 3 sc in ch-2 sp,
sc in next 9 sps, sl st in last st; fasten
off.

Edging
Note: Work rows 1 and 2 of edging
for 7 Panels, then work row 1 only
for 1 Panel and row 2 only for rem
Panel.
Row 1 (rs): With rs facing and using
crochet hook, join MC in top left
corner with sl st, ch 1, sc in same st,
work 213 sc evenly across to next
corner, 2 sc in corner; fasten off:
216 sc.

(continued)

Row 2 (rs): With rs facing and using crochet hook, join MC in bottom right corner with sl st, ch 1, sc in same st, work 213 sc evenly across to next corner, 2 sc in corner; fasten off: 216 sc.

Assembly

Referring to **Assembly Diagram,** turn every other panel upside down, with panels with unfinished edges to outside. Join 2 panels as folls: With ws tog and using crochet hook, join MC in top corner with sl st, ch 1, working in both lps, sc in same sc and in ea sc across; fasten off. Rep to join all panels.

Border

Rnd 1 (rs): With rs facing and using crochet hook, join MC in bottom left corner with sl st, ch 1, 3 sc in same st, (sc in ea st across to next joining, sc in joining, sc in ea st across to next point, 3 sc in point, sc in ea st across to next joining, sc in joining) 4 times, sc in ea st across to next joining, sc in joining, sc in ea st across to corner, 3 sc in corner, sc in ea st across to next corner, 3 sc in corner, (sc in ea st across to next point, 3 sc in point, sc in ea st across to next joining, sc in joining, sc in ea st across to next joining, sc in joining) 4 times, sc in ea st across to next point, 3 sc in point, sc in ea st across to corner, 3 sc in corner, sc in ea st across to next corner; join with sl st to beg sc.

Rnd 2 (ws): Ch 1, turn; working in bk lps only, sc in ea sc around; sl st to beg ch-1; do not fasten off.

Rnd 3 (rs): Ch 1, turn; working in unused lps of row 1, 3 sc in same st, (sc in ea sc across to next V, sk 2 sc, sc in ea sc across to next point, 3 sc in point) 4 times, sc in ea sc across to next V, sk 2 sc, sc in ea sc across to next corner, 3 sc in corner, (sc in ea sc across to next point, 3 sc in point, sc in ea sc across to next V, sk 2 sc) 4 times, sc in ea sc across to next point, 3 sc in point, sc in ea sc across to next corner, 3 sc in corner, sc in ea sc across to next corner; join with sl st to beg sc; fasten off.

Rnd 4 (rs): With rs facing, join A in bottom left corner with sl st, ch 1, 3 sc in same st, (sc in ea sc across to next V, sk 2 sc, sc in ea sc across to next point, 3 sc in point) 4 times, sc in ea sc across to next V, sk 2 sc, sc in ea sc across to next corner, 3 sc in corner, (sc in ea sc across to next point, 3 sc in point, sc in ea sc across to next V, sk 2 sc) 4 times, sc in ea sc across to next point, 3 sc in point, sc in ea sc across to next corner, 3 sc in corner, sc in ea sc across to next corner; join with sl st to beg sc; fasten off.

Rnds 5–10: Rep row 4, 6 times, foll color sequence: 1 row ea F, E, D, C, B, MC; do not fasten off after last row.

Rnd 11: Sl st in first sc and in ea sc around; join with sl st to beg sl st; fasten off.

Afghan by Karen Nagle, Auburn, Pennsylvania

Assembly Diagram

Baby Blocks

Knit this cozy blanket in simple stockinette stitch for a quick shower gift. Embellish it with lazy-daisy flowers and duplicate stitch.

Materials

Worsted-weight acrylic yarn,
    approximately:
7 oz. (400 yd.) white, MC
3½ oz. (200 yd.) blue, A
3½ oz. (200 yd.) yellow, B
3½ oz. (200 yd.) pink, C
3½ oz. (200 yd.) green, D
Size 8 circular knitting needles
    or size to obtain gauge
Yarn needle

Finished Size

Approximately 31" x 35"

Gauge

In St st, 18 sts and 26 rows = 4"

Note: To change colors, pick up new color from beneath old color, holding old color snugly to avoid holes. Do not carry yarn across row.

With MC, CO 154 sts.
Rows 1–5: K across.
Row 6 (rs): K 5, change to A, k 36, change to B, k 36, change to C, k 36, change to D, k 36, change to MC, k 5.
Row 7: K 5, change to D, p 36, change to C, p 36, change to B, p 36, change to A, p 36, change to MC, k 5.
Rows 8–53: Work in St st for 46 rows, changing colors as est.
Row 54: K 5, change to C, k 36, change to MC, k 72, change to B, k 36, change to MC, k 5.
Row 55: K 5, change to B, p 36, change to MC, p 72, change to C, p 36, change to MC, k 5.
Rows 56–101: Work in St st for 46 rows, changing colors as est.
Row 102: K 5, change to D, k 36, change to MC, k 72, change to A, k 36, change to MC, k 5.

Row 103: K 5, change to A, p 36, change to MC, p 72, change to D, p 36, change to MC, k 5.
Rows 104–149: Work in St st for 46 rows, changing colors as est.
Row 150: K 5, change to B, k 36, change to A, k 36, change to D, k 36, change to C, k 36, change to MC, k 5.
Row 151: K 5, change to C, p 36, change to D, p 36, change to A, p 36, change to B, p 36, change to MC, k 5.
Rows 152–197: Work in St st for 46 rows, changing colors as est.
Rows 198–202: K across; BO.

Duplicate Stitch

Referring to page 158 of General Directions and foll *Chart,* duplicate-stitch letters. Referring to photo, embroider flowers and leaves, using 1"-long lazy-daisy stitches.

*Afghan by Linda Roper
Richmond, Virginia*

Key

☐	MC
☒	A
⬤	B
○	C
⊞	D

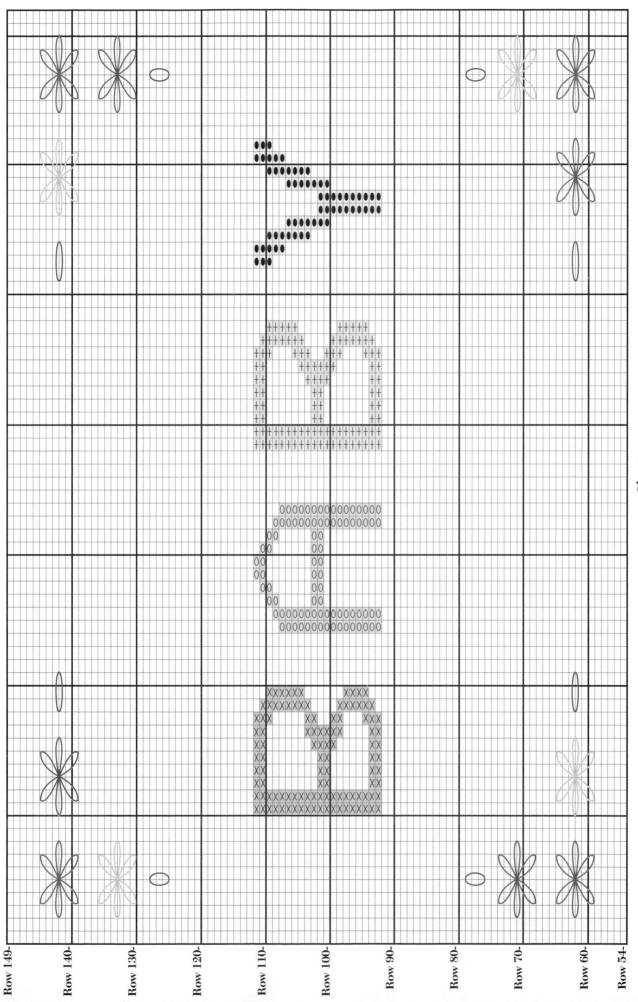

Chart

141

Row 149-
Row 140-
Row 130-
Row 120-
Row 110-
Row 100-
Row 90-
Row 80-
Row 70-
Row 60-
Row 54-

Puffed Stripes

Pastel puffs accent each colored stripe.

Materials

Worsted-weight brushed acrylic yarn, approximately:
24½ oz. (1,470 yd.) white, MC
3½ oz. (210 yd.) blue, A
3½ oz. (210 yd.) green, B
3½ oz. (210 yd.) yellow, C
3½ oz. (210 yd.) peach, D
3½ oz. (210 yd.) pink, E
Size I crochet hook or size to obtain gauge

Finished Size

Approximately 34" x 40", without fringe

Gauge

13 sc and 16 rows = 4"

Pattern Stitch

Puff: (Yo, insert hook in st indicated, yo and pull up lp) 4 times, yo and pull through all 9 lps on hook, ch 1.

Note: To change colors, work last yo of prev st with new color, dropping prev color to ws of work. Do not carry yarn across row.

With MC, ch 110.
Row 1 (rs): Sc in 2nd ch from hook and in ea ch across: 109 sc.
Rows 2–4: Ch 1, turn; sc in ea st across, change to A after last row: 109 sc.
Row 5: Rep row 2; do not change colors.
Row 6: Ch 1, turn; sc in next 3 sc, * puff in next sc, sc in next 5 sc; rep from * across to last 4 sc, puff in next sc, sc in next 3 sc, change to MC: 18 puffs.
Rows 7–10: Rep row 2, 4 times, change to B after last row.
Row 11: Rep row 2; do not change colors.
Row 12: Ch 1, turn; sc in next 6 sc, * puff in next sc, sc in next 5 sc; rep from * across to last sc, sc in last sc: 17 puffs.

Rows 13–16: Rep row 2, 4 times, change to C after last row.
Rows 17 and 18: Rep rows 5 and 6.
Rows 19–22: Rep row 2, 4 times, change to D after last row.
Rows 23 and 24: Rep rows 11 and 12.
Rows 25–28: Rep row 2, 4 times, change to E after last row.
Rows 29 and 30: Rep rows 5 and 6.
Rows 31–36: Rep rows 19–24 once.
Rows 37–42: Rep rows 13–18 once.
Rows 43–48: Rep rows 7–12 once.
Rows 49–54: Rep row 2 once, then rep rows 2–6 once.
Rows 55–154: Rep rows 7–54 twice, then rep row 2, 4 times; do not fasten off.

Border

Rnd 1 (rs): Ch 1, turn; 2 sc in first sc, sc in ea sc across to next corner, * 3 sc in corner, sc evenly across to next corner; rep from * around, sc in corner; join with sl st to beg sc.
Rnd 2 (rs): Ch 1, do not turn; working from left to right, sc in joining, * ch 1, sk 1 sc, sc in next sc; rep from * around; join with sl st to beg sc; fasten off.

Fringe

For ea tassel, referring to page 159 of General Directions, cut 8 (12") lengths MC. Working across short ends, knot 1 tassel in every other ch-1 sp.

Afghan by Monica Kancel-Costello, Hannibal, Ohio

General Directions

A Note to Left-handed Crocheters and Knitters

Instructions for projects most often appear with instructions for right-handers only, so it may be worthwhile to learn these techniques. Since yarn work is shared between the hands, you may find it surprisingly easy for you to use the accompanying diagrams. If working in this way is not comfortable, use a mirror to reverse the diagrams or reverse them on a photocopier.

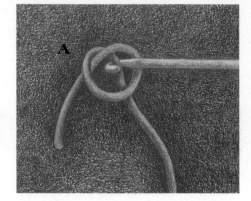

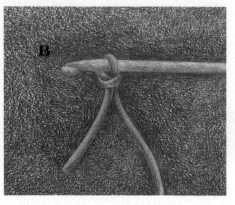

Slip Knot

A. Loop yarn around and let loose end of yarn fall behind loop to form pretzel shape as shown. Insert hook or needle.

B. Pull both ends of yarn to close knot.

Chart

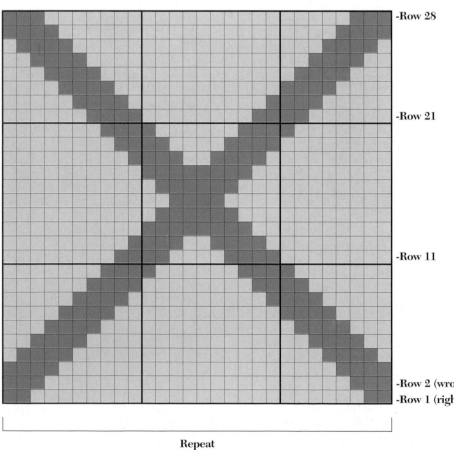

-Row 28

-Row 21

-Row 11

-Row 2 (wrong-side row)
-Row 1 (right-side row)

Repeat

Gauge

Before beginning a project, work a 4"-square gauge swatch, using the recommended size hook or needles. Count and compare the number of stitches per inch in the swatch with the designer's gauge. If you have fewer stitches in your swatch, try a smaller hook or needle; if you have more stitches, try a larger hook or needle.

Reading Charts

Sometimes charts are easier to follow than lengthy directions (see **Chart** at left). Each square on this chart represents one stitch. Usually, charts are read from bottom to top, right to left for right-side rows and left to right for wrong-side rows.

Crochet Directions

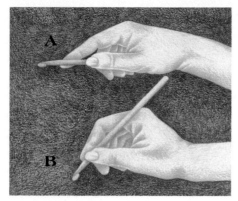

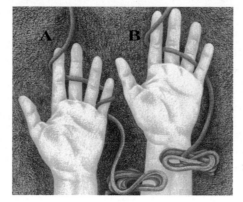

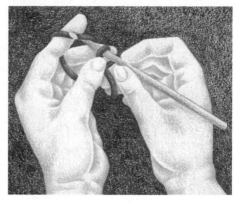

Holding the Hook
Hold the hook as you would a piece of chalk (**A**) or a pencil (**B**). If your hook has a finger rest, position your thumb and opposing finger there for extra control.

Holding the Yarn
Weave the yarn through the fingers of your left hand. Some people like to wrap the yarn around the little finger for extra control (**A**); some do not (**B**). In either case, the forefinger plays the most important role in regulating tension as yarn is fed into the work.

Working Together
Once work has begun, the thumb and the middle finger of the left hand come into play, pressing together to hold the stitches just made.

Crochet Abbreviations

beg	begin(ning)	FP	front post	sp(s)	space(s)
bet	between	ft lp(s)	front loop(s)	st(s)	stitch(es)
bk lp(s)	back loop(s)	grp(s)	group(s)	tch	turning chain
BP	back post	hdc	half double crochet	tog	together
ch	chain(s)	inc	increas(es) (ed) (ing)	tr	triple crochet
ch-	refers to chain previously made	lp(s)	loop(s)	ws	wrong side
cl	cluster(s)	pat(s)	pattern(s)	yo	yarn over
cont	continu(e) (ing)	prev	previous		
dc	double crochet	rem	remain(s) (ing)		
dec	decreas(es) (ed) (ing)	rep	repeat(s)		
dtr	double triple crochet	rnd(s)	round(s)		
ea	each	rs	right side		
est	established	sc	single crochet		
foll	follow(s) (ing)	sk	skip(ped)		
		sl st	slip stitch		

Repeat whatever follows * as indicated. "Rep from * 3 times" means to work 4 times in all.

Work directions given in parentheses ( ) and brackets [ ] the number of times specified or in the place specified.

Crochet Hook Sizes

U.S.	Size	Metric	Canada/U.K.	U.S.	Size	Metric	Canada/U.K.	U.S.	Size	Metric	Canada/U.K.
B	(1)	2.25	13	F	(5)	4.00	—	J	(10)	6.00	4
C	(2)	2.75	—	G	(6)	4.25	8	K	(10½)	6.50	3
D	(3)	3.25	10	H	(8)	5.00	6	N	—	10.00	000
E	(4)	3.50	9	I	(9)	5.50	5				

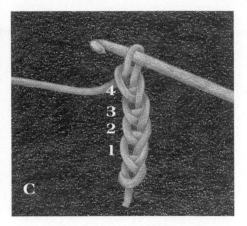

Chain Stitch

A. Place slip knot on hook. With thumb and middle finger of left hand holding yarn end, wrap yarn up and over hook (from back to front). This movement is called "yarn over (yo)" and is basic to every crochet stitch.

B. Use hook to pull yarn through loop (lp) already on hook. Combination of yo and pulling yarn through lp makes 1 chain stitch (ch).

C. Repeat A and B until ch is desired length. Try to keep movements even and relaxed and all ch stitches (sts) same size. Hold ch near working area to keep it from twisting. Count sts as shown in diagram. (Do not count lp on hook or slip knot.)

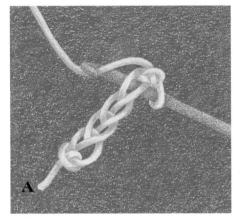

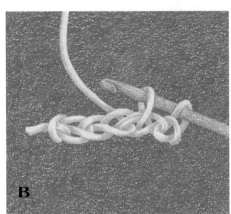

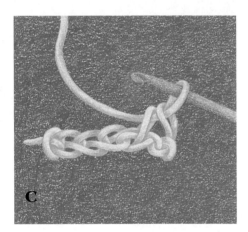

Single Crochet

A. Insert hook under top 2 lps of 2nd ch from hook and yo. (Always work sts through top 2 lps unless directions specify otherwise.)

B. Yo and pull yarn through ch (2 lps on hook).

C. Yo and pull yarn through 2 lps on hook [1 sc made].

Slip Stitch

Here slip stitch (sl st) is used to join ring. Taking care not to twist chain, insert hook into first ch made, yo and pull through ch and lp on hook [sl st made]. Sl st can also be used to join finished pieces or to move across groups of sts without adding height to work.

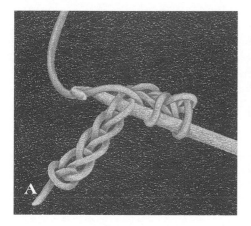

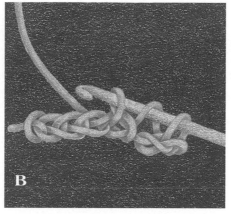

Double Crochet

A. Yo, insert hook into 4th ch from hook, and yo.

B. Yo and pull yarn through ch (3 lps on hook).

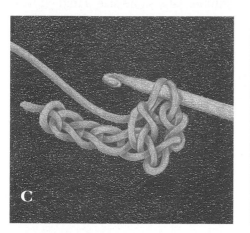

C. Yo and pull through 2 lps on hook (2 lps remaining [rem]).

D. Yo and pull through 2 rem lps [1 dc made].

Joining Yarn or Changing Colors

To change colors or to begin a new skein of yarn at the end of a row, work the last yarn over for the last stitch of the previous row with the new yarn.

Fastening Off

Cut the yarn, leaving a 6" tail. Yarn over and pull the tail through the last loop on the hook. Thread the tail into a large-eyed yarn needle and weave it carefully into the back of the work.

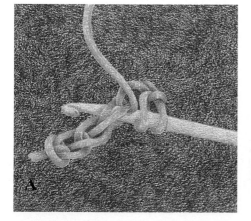

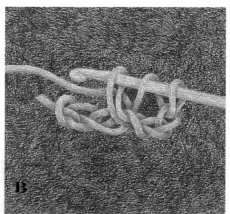

Half Double Crochet

A. Yo and insert hook into 3rd ch from hook.

B. Yo and pull through ch (3 lps on hook).

C. Yo and pull yarn through all 3 lps on hook [1 hdc made].

147

Triple Crochet

A. Yo twice, insert hook into 5th ch from hook. Yo and pull through ch (4 lps on hook).

B. Yo and pull through 2 lps on hook (3 lps rem). Yo and pull through 2 lps on hook (2 lps rem). Yo and pull through 2 lps on hook [1 tr made].

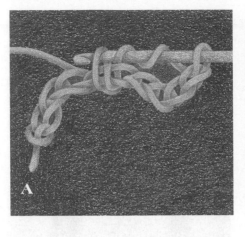

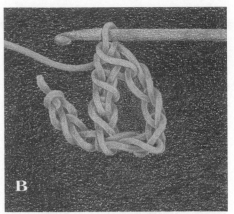

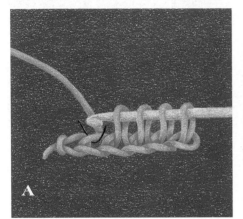

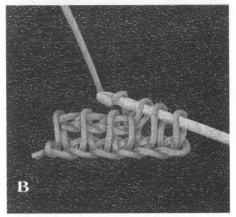

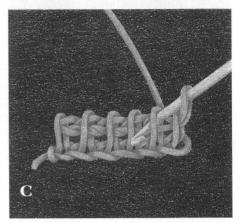

Afghan Stitch

A. *Row 1: Step 1:* Keeping all lps on hook, pull up lp through top lp only in 2nd ch from hook and in ea ch across = same number of lps and chs. Do not turn.

B. *Step 2:* Yo and pull through first lp on hook, * yo and pull through 2 lps on hook, rep from * across (1 lp rem on hook for first lp of next row). Do not turn.

C. *Row 2: Step 1:* Keeping all lps on hook, pull up lp from under 2nd vertical bar, * pull up lp from under next vertical bar, rep from * across. Do not turn. *Step 2:* Rep step 2 of row 1.

Rep both steps of row 2 for required number of rows. Fasten off after last row by working sl st in ea bar across.

Front Post dc (FPdc)

A. Yo and insert hook from front to back around post of st on previous row.

B. Complete dc st as usual. (Back post dc [BPdc] is worked in same manner, except you insert hook from back to front around post.)

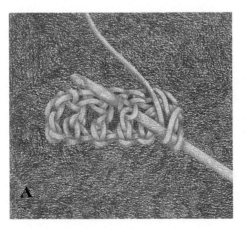

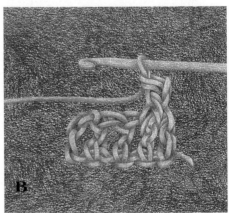

Stitch Placement Variations

Working in Back Loops Only

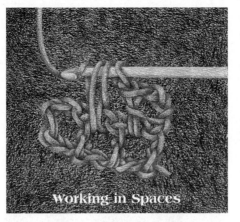
Working in Spaces

Working Between Stitches

Basic Popcorn
A. Work 5 dc in st indicated, drop lp from hook and insert hook in first dc of 5-dc grp.
B. Pick up dropped lp and pull through.

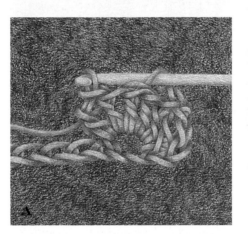
A

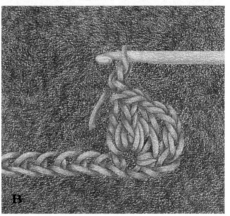
B

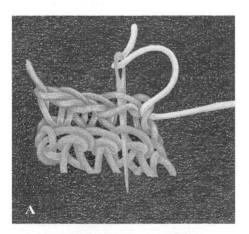
A

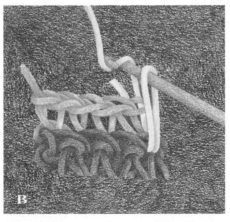
B

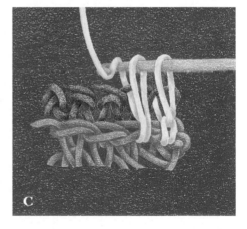
C

Assembly
To assemble crocheted pieces, use a large-eyed yarn needle to whipstitch (**A**) or a crochet hook to slip stitch (**B**) the pieces together. Pieces can also be joined using single crochet stitches (**C**), but this makes a heavier seam.

When making squares or other pieces to be stitched together, leave a long tail of yarn when fastening off. This yarn tail can then be used to stitch the pieces together. Be sure all stitches and rows of the squares or the strips are aligned and running in the same direction.

Knit Directions

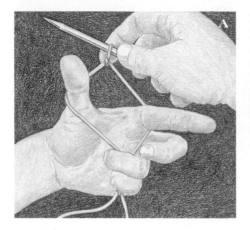

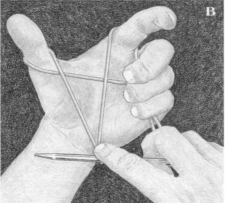

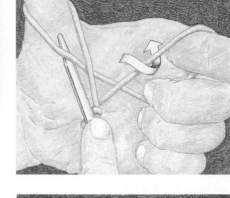

Casting On

Measure 1" of yarn for each stitch (st) to be cast on. For example, measure 30" to cast on 30 sts. Make slip knot at this measurement. Place slip knot on needle (counts as 1 st).

A. Holding needle with slip knot in right hand with index finger resting on slip knot, place yarn tail in back of left thumb and working yarn in back of left index finger. Hold both yarn strands with remaining fingers.

B. Bring needle down so that yarn forms V between left thumb and index finger.

C. Insert needle from bottom through thumb loop.

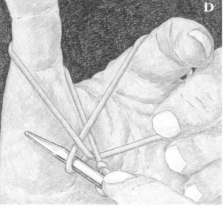

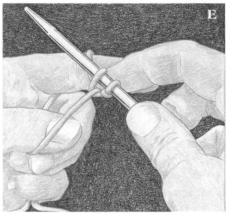

D. Insert needle from top through index finger loop and pull through thumb loop.

E. Slip thumb out of loop and tighten stitch around needle. Repeat steps C–E until you have required number of stitches on needle. Each loop (lp) on needle counts as 1 st.

Holding the Yarn for Knitting

Weave the yarn through the fingers of your right hand. Some people like to wrap the yarn around the little finger or the index finger for extra control. The forefinger plays the most important role in regulating tension as yarn is fed into the work.

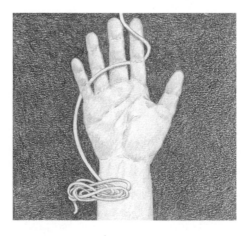

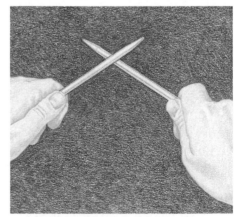

Holding the Knitting Needles

Hold the needles overhand, similar to how you would hold a piece of chalk.

Knit Abbreviations

beg	begin(ning)	k2tog	knit 2 stitches together	tog	together
bet	between	p	purl	ws	wrong side
BO	bind off	p2tog	purl 2 stitches together	yb	bring yarn to back
CB	cable back	pat(s)	pattern(s)	yf	bring yarn to front
CF	cable front	prev	previous	yo	yarn over
CO	cast on	psso	pass slipped stitch over		
cont	continu(e) (ing)	rem	remain(s) (ing)		
dec	decreas(es) (ed) (ing)	rep	repeat(s)		
ea	each	rs	right side		
est	established	sk	skip(ped)		
foll	follow(s) (ing)	sl	slip		
inc	increas(es) (ed) (ing)	st(s)	stitch(es)		
k	knit	St st	stockinette stitch		

Repeat whatever follows * as indicated. "Rep from * 3 times" means to work 4 times in all.

Work directions given in parentheses ( ) and brackets [ ] the number of times specified or in the place specified.

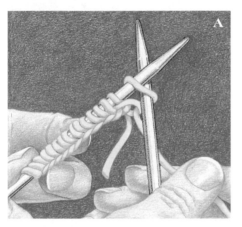

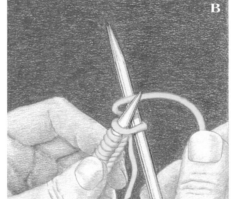

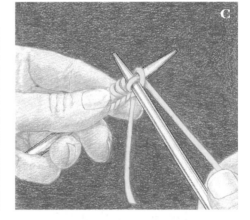

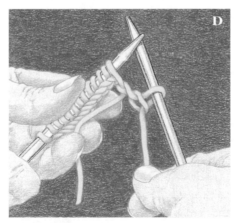

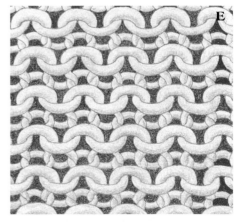

Knit

Hold needle with sts in left hand and empty needle in right hand

A. With yarn in back of needles, insert right needle in front of first st on left needle from left to right.

B. Wrap yarn from back to front around right needle.

C. Bring right needle back through st on left needle, pulling loop through st.

D. Slip (sl) st off left needle [1 k st made].

E. Rep steps A–D across until all sts are on right needle to complete 1 row of knitting. Return needle with sts to left hand and rep steps A–E again. When every row is worked as a knit row, it is called *garter stitch*.

Knitting Needle Sizes

U.S.	Metric	Canada/U.K.	U.S.	Metric	Canada/U.K.	U.S.	Metric	Canada/U.K.
0	2.00	13	6	4.25	7	11	8.00	1
1	2.25	12	7	4.50	6	13	9.00	00
2	2.75	11	8	5.00	5	15	10.00	000
3	3.25	10	9	5.50	4	17	12.00	—
4	3.50	9	10	6.00	3	19	15.00	—
5	3.75	8	10½	6.50	2	35	20.00	—

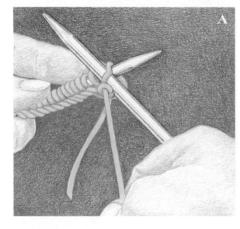

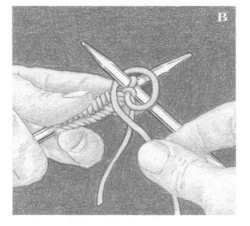

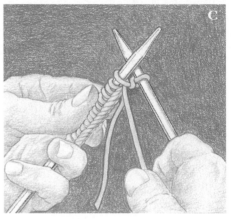

Purl

Hold needle with sts in left hand and empty needle in right hand.

A. With yarn in front of needles, insert right needle in front of first st on left needle from right to left.

B. Wrap yarn from front to back around right needle.

C. Bring right needle back through st on left needle, pulling loop through st.

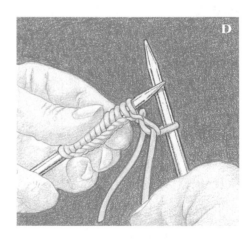

D. Sl st off left needle [1 p st made].

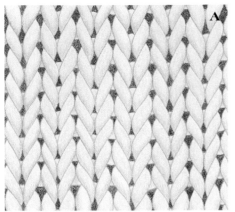

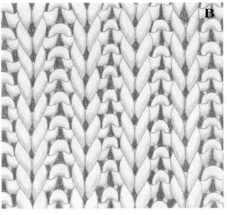

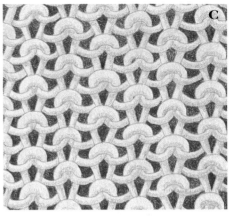

| Stockinette Stitch | Ribbing | Seed Stitch |

Combining Knit and Purl Stitches

You can combine k and p for several basic st patterns.

Stockinette Stitch

Row 1: K across.

Row 2: P across.

Rep rows 1 and 2 alternately.

Ribbing

K 1, p 1, across ea row. (You will k ea k st and p ea p st.)

Seed Stitch

Row 1: K 1, p 1, across.

Row 2: P 1, k 1 across.

Rep rows 1 and 2 alternately. (You will k ea p st and p ea k st.)

Slip Stitch

As if to k, insert right needle in front of first st on left needle from left to right. Sl stitch off left needle [sl st made].

As if to p, insert right needle in front of first st on left needle from right to left. Sl st off left needle [sl st made].

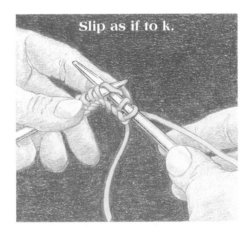

Slip as if to k.

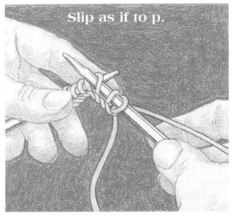

Slip as if to p.

Decreasing

There are several ways to decrease (dec) sts, depending on which way the sts need to slant.

Knit 2 Together

A. With yarn in back of needles, insert right needle in front of first 2 sts on left needle from left to right. Wrap yarn from back to front around right needle.

B. Bring right needle back through both sts on left needle, pulling loop through st. Sl sts off left needle [1 dec made]. Dec slants to right on k side of work.

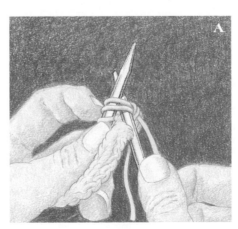

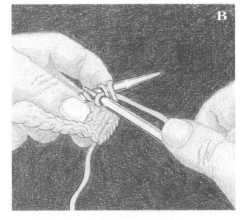

153

Purl 2 Together

A. With yarn in front of needles, insert right needle in front of first 2 sts on left needle from right to left. Wrap yarn from front to back around right needle.

B. Bring right needle back through both sts on left needle, pulling loop through st. Sl sts off left needle [1 dec made]. Dec slants to right on k side of work.

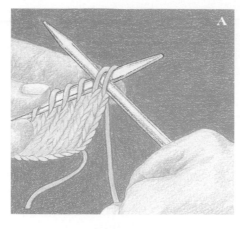
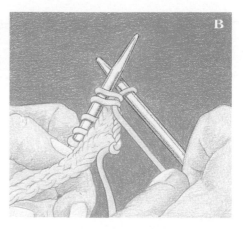

Knit 2 Together in Back

A. With yarn in back of needles, insert right needle in back of first 2 sts on left needle from right to left. Wrap yarn from back to front around right needle.

B. Bring right needle back through both sts on left needle, pulling loop through st. Sl sts off left needle [1 dec made]. Dec slants to left on k side of work.

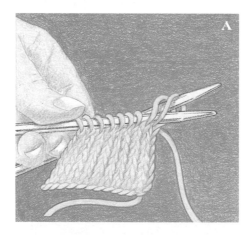
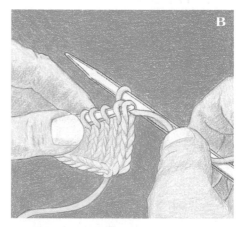

Purl 2 Together in Back

A. With yarn in front of needles, insert right needle in back of first 2 sts on left needle from left to right. Wrap yarn from front to back around right needle.

B. Bring right needle back through both sts on left needle, pulling loop through st. Sl sts off left needle [1 dec made]. Dec slants to left on k side of work.

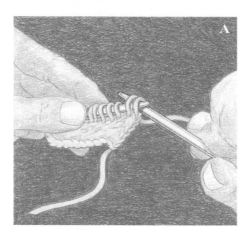
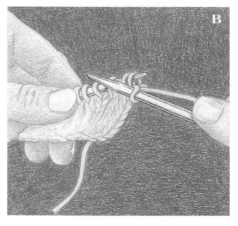

Pass Slipped Stitch Over (psso)

Slip 1 stitch and complete the next stitch. With the tip of the left needle, bring the slipped stitch on the right needle over the last stitch on the right needle (**A**) and off both needles (**B**) [decrease made]. The decrease slants to the left on the knit side of the work.

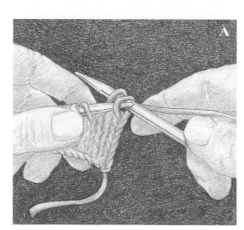
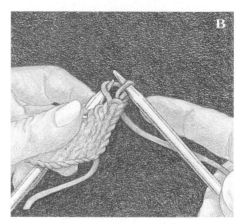

Increasing

There are also several ways to increase (inc) stitches, depending on the desired effect.

Yarn Over

A. With yarn in back of needles, wrap yarn counterclockwise around right needle, then insert right needle in next st on left needle as if to k.
B. Complete k st [inc made]. Inc creates hole.

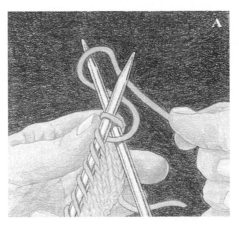

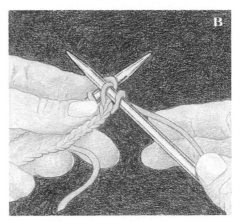

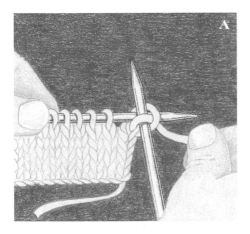

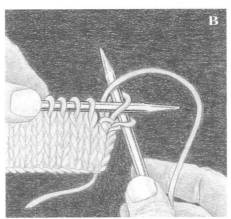

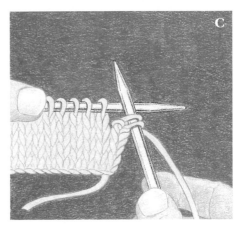

Knit in Front and Back of Stitch

A. Work k st, but do not sl st off needle.

B. Insert right needle in back of same st on left needle from right to left. Wrap yarn from back to front around right needle.

C. Bring right needle back through st on left needle, pulling loop through st. Sl st off left needle [inc made]. Inc creates small horizontal bar on k side of work.

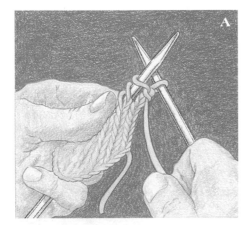

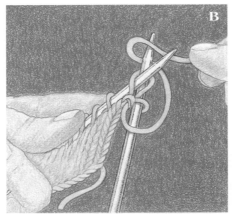

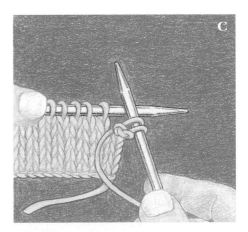

Purl in Front and Back of Stitch

A. Work p st, but do not sl st off needle.

B. Insert right needle in back of same st on left needle from left to right. Wrap yarn from front to back around right needle.

C. Bring right needle back through st on left needle, pulling loop through st. Sl st off left needle [inc made]. Inc creates small horizontal bar on k side of work.

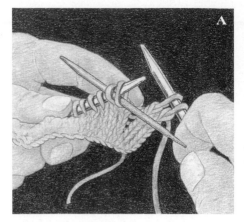

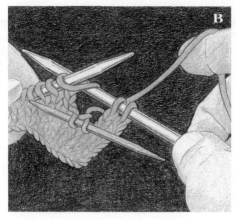

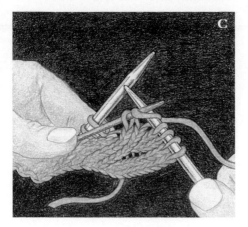

Basic Cable
You will need a cable needle in addition to knitting needles.

A. Sl specified number of sts as if to p from left needle onto cable needle.

B. To cable front (CF, see below), hold cable needle in front of work and k specified number of sts from left needle.

C. K sts from cable needle.

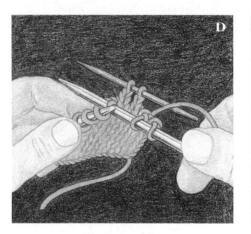

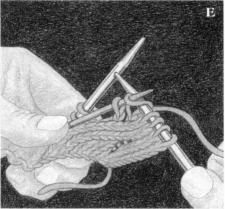

D. To cable back (CB, see below), hold cable needle in back of work and k specified number of sts from left needle.

E. K sts from cable needle.

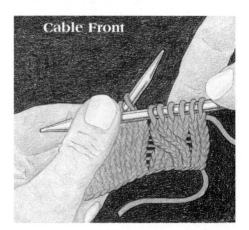

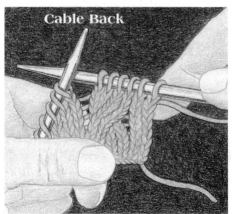

Dropped Stitches

If you drop a stitch, use a crochet hook to pick it back up.

A. Insert hook in dropped stitch, pick up strand above stitch, and pull strand through loop on hook.

B. Continue until loop on hook is even with stitches on needle. Slip stitch from hook onto left needle with right side of stitch to front.

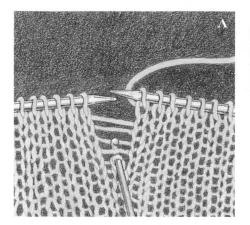
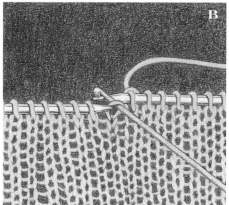

Changing Colors

To change colors, pick up the new color from beneath the old color, holding the old color snugly to avoid holes.

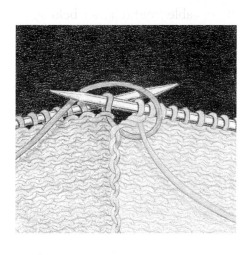

Joining Yarn

To begin a new skein of yarn at the beginning of a row, cut off the old yarn, leaving a 6" tail. Beginning with a 6" tail, use the new yarn to work the next stitch. If desired, tie the yarn tails together temporarily with a single knot. Untie and weave the tails into the seams later.

Binding Off

Always bind off loosely.

A. K 2 sts. With tip of left needle, bring first st on right needle over next st on right needle and off both needles [1 st bound off].

B. K next st. With tip of left needle, bring first st on right needle over next st on right needle and off both needles [1 st bound off]. Cont across to last st. Cut yarn, leaving long tail. Pull tail through last st and tighten.

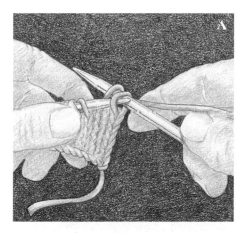
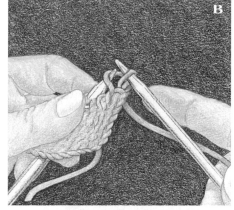

Metric Math

When you know:	Multiply by:	To find:	When you know:	Multiply by:	To find:
inches (")	25	millimeters (mm)	millimeters (mm)	0.039	inches (")
inches (")	2.5	centimeters (cm)	centimeters (cm)	0.39	inches (")
inches (")	0.025	meters (m)	meters (m)	39	inches (")
yards (yd.)	0.9	meters (m)	meters (m)	1.093	yards (yd.)
ounces (oz.)	28.35	grams (g)	grams (g)	0.035	ounces (oz.)

Duplicate Stitch

A. Thread yarn needle with contrasting color. Bring needle up at base of st and insert needle under base of next st.

B. Insert needle at base of st (where you began). Contrasting color should cover original st. Keep tension of sts even to avoid puckering. Weave in tails to secure.

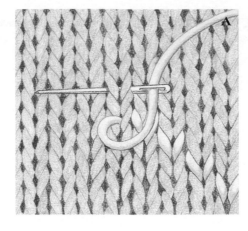

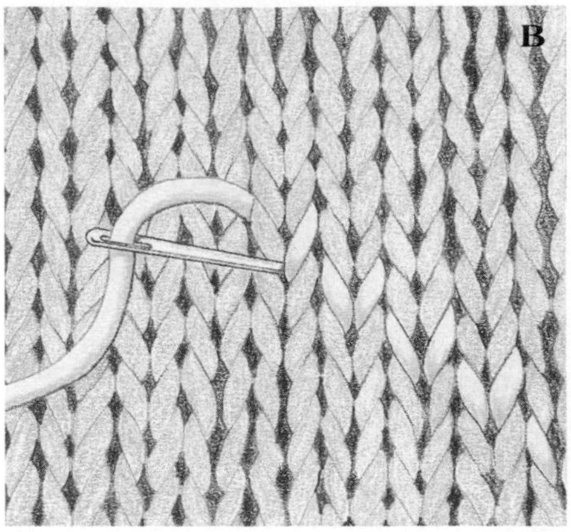

Assembly

To assemble knitted pieces, use a large-eyed yarn needle to whipstitch the pieces together (**A**).

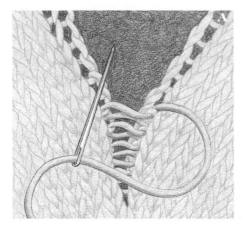

To weave the pieces together, as in *Fan-Stitch Favorite* on page 44, with the right sides of both pieces up, sew through both sides once to

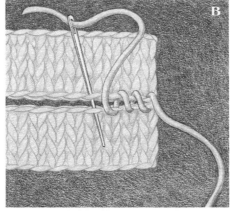

secure the beginning of the seam. Insert the needle under the bar between the first and second stitches on the first row and pull the needle through. Insert the needle under the next bar on the second side (**B**). Continue in this manner, keeping rows aligned and pulling gently on the yarn to keep the seam elastic.

When making squares or other pieces to be stitched together, leave a long tail of yarn when fastening off. This yarn tail can then be used to stitch the pieces together. Be sure all stitches and rows of the squares or the strips are aligned and running in the same direction.

Metric Conversion

⅛" = 3 mm	5" = 12.7 cm	⅛ yard = 0.11 m
¼" = 6 mm	6" = 15.2 cm	¼ yard = 0.23 m
⅜" = 9 mm	7" = 17.8 cm	⅓ yard = 0.3 m
½" = 1.3 cm	8" = 20.3 cm	⅜ yard = 0.34 m
⅝" = 1.6 cm	9" = 22.9 cm	½ yard = 0.46 m
¾" = 1.9 cm	10" = 25.4 cm	⅝ yard = 0.57 m
⅞" = 2.2 cm	11" = 27.9 cm	⅔ yard = 0.61 m
1" = 2.5 cm	12" = 30.5 cm	¾ yard = 0.69 m
2" = 5.1 cm	36" = 91.5 cm	⅞ yard = 0.8 m
3" = 7.6 cm	45" = 114.3 cm	1 yard = 0.91 m
4" = 10.2 cm	60" = 152.4 cm	

Finishing Touches

Lazy Daisy

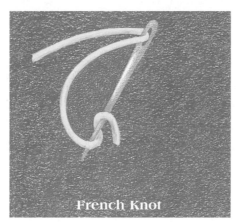

French Knot

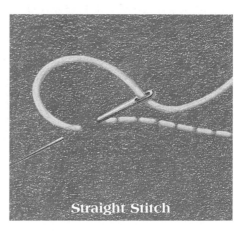

Straight Stitch

Embroidery Stitches
Thread a large-eyed yarn needle to embellish a crocheted or knitted piece with embroidery. Weave in the yarn tails; do not use knots.

A

B

C

D

E

Fringe
To make a simple fringe, cut the required number of yarn lengths as specified in the directions. Insert the hook through 1 stitch at the edge of the afghan and fold the yarn lengths in half over the hook (**A**). Pull the folded yarn partway through the stitch to form a loop (**B**). Pull the yarn ends through the loop (**C**) and pull tight (**D**). To double-knot the fringe, divide each tassel in half. Knot the halves of 2 adjacent tassels together about 1" below the top row of knots (**E**).

Index

Abbreviations
  crochet, 145
  knit, 151
Afghan stitch (crochet), 148
Afghan-stitch afghans
  Afghan-Stitch Aran, 58
  Artful Aztec, 46
  Bargello Beauty, 66
  Bluebirds and Bluebells, 32
  Borderline, 76
  Cheyenne Chevron, 84
  Christmas Celebration, 70
  Heavenly Love, 106
  Hummingbirds, 88
  Paisley Perfection, 55
  Rainbow Ripple, 136
  Stained Glass, 100
  Tic-tac-toe, 122
Aran-style afghans
  Afghan-Stitch Aran, 58
  Colorful Cables, 97
  Cowboy Blues, 94
  Diamonds and Rings, 61
  Irish Trellis, 50
  Pretty in Pink, 86
  Textured Sampler, 27
Assembly
  crochet, 149
  knit, 158
Baby afghans
  Baby Blocks, 139
  Color Block, 120
  Filet Hearts, 129
  Giraffes, 110
  Pink and Blue, 118
  Puffed Shells, 134
  Puffed Stripes, 142
  Rainbow Ripple, 136
  Sherbet Stripes, 132
  Spots and Stripes, 126
  Tweed Stripes, 116
  White Shells, 114
Back post double crochet stitch, 148
Binding off (knit), 157
Cable (knit), 156
Casting on (knit), 150
Chain stitch (crochet), 146
Changing colors
  crochet, 147
  knit, 157
Charts, reading, 144
Decreasing (knit), 153–154
Double crochet stitch, 147

Dropped stitches, (knit), 157
Duplicate stitch (knit), 158
Embroidery stitches, 159
Fastening off yarn
  crochet, 147
  knit, 157
Fringe, 159
Front post double crochet stitch, 148
Garter stitch (knit), 151
Gauge, 144
Granny square variations
  Blue Star, 16
  Floral Fantasy, 37
  Garden Rows, 4
  Groovy Granny, 7
  Memory Star, 24
  Mum's the Word, 40
Half-double crochet stitch, 147
Hook sizes (crochet), 145
Increasing (knit), 155
Joining yarn
  crochet, 147
  knit, 157
Knit stitch, 151
Knitted afghans
  Baby Blocks, 139
  Colorful Cables, 97
  Fan-Stitch Favorite, 44
  Hearts and Flowers, 73
  Spots and Stripes, 126
Needle sizes (knit), 152
One-piece afghans
  Baby Blocks, 139
  Bright Ribbons, 82
  Cheyenne Chevron, 84
  Color Block, 120
  Colorful Cables, 97
  Cowboy Blues, 94
  Filet Hearts, 129
  Giraffes, 110
  Hearts and Flowers, 73
  Irish Trellis, 50
  Lattice, 80
  Pink and Blue, 118
  Pretty in Pink, 86
  Puffed Shells, 134
  Puffed Stripes, 142
  Purple Starbursts, 42
  Rippling Shells, 64
  Sandy Shells, 10
  Scalloped Ripple, 52
  Sherbet Stripes, 132
  Textured Sampler, 27

Tic-tac-toe, 122
Tumbling Blocks, 92
Tweed Stripes, 116
White Shells, 114
Panel afghans
  Afghan-Stitch Aran, 58
  Artful Aztec, 46
  Bargello Beauty, 66
  Bluebirds and Bluebells, 32
  Borderline, 76
  Christmas Celebration, 70
  Diamonds and Rings, 61
  Fan-Stitch Favorite, 44
  Heavenly Love, 106
  Hummingbirds, 88
  Paisley Perfection, 55
  Pink Diamonds, 30
  Rainbow Ripple, 136
  Stained Glass, 100
Pieced afghans
  Blue Star, 16
  Country Quilt, 12
  Floral Fantasy, 37
  Garden Rows, 4
  Groovy Granny, 7
  Memory Star, 24
  Mum's the Word, 40
  Pinwheel, 22
  Spots and Stripes, 126
Popcorn stitch (crochet), 149
Purl stitch (knit), 152
Ribbing stitch (knit), 153
Ripple stitch afghans
  Fan-Stitch Favorite, 44
  Rainbow Ripple, 136
  Rippling Shells, 64
  Scalloped Ripple, 52
Seed stitch (knit), 153
Shell stitch afghans
  Pink and Blue, 118
  Puffed Shells, 134
  Rippling Shells, 64
  Sandy Shells, 10
  Sherbet Stripes, 132
  White Shells, 114
Single crochet stitch, 146
Slip knot, 144
Slip stitch
  crochet, 146
  knit, 153
Stockinette stitch (knit), 153
Triple crochet stitch, 148